# TRANSFORM
## YOUR WORK LIFE

Copyright 2011 by Graham Power and Dion Forster

Published in Boise, Idaho by Russell Media
Web: http://www.russell-media.com
This book may be purchased in bulk for educational, business, or promotional use.
For information please email customerservice@russell-media.com

To learn more about personal finance, the author, or seminars based on the content contained in this book, please
go to http://www.unashamedlyethical.com

ISBN (print):          978-0-9829300-7-6
ISBN (e-book):         978-0-9829300-8-3

Cover design and layout by Brandon Hill.

Originally published by Struik Christian Media in South Africa.

Printed in the United States of America.

Power, Graham and Forster, Dion
  Transform Your Work Life: Turn Your Ordinary Day into an Extraordinary Calling


Library of Congress Control Number: 2011929127

# TRANSFORM YOUR WORK LIFE

TURN YOUR ORDINARY DAY INTO AN EXTRAORDINARY CALLING

GRAHAM POWER *AND* DION FORSTER

At long last we have a book that affirms our daily workplace as a primary place for us to live out our faith. Few people are better placed and more equipped to show us the way than Dion Forster and Graham Power. I pray that this book will enable many individuals the world over to see their work as a means of dignity, love and provision, both for themselves and their neighbour.

– Rev Trevor Hudson, South African Pastor and Author

For many centuries there has been an unfortunate separation in the minds of Christians between calling and vocation. In the last twenty years this has changed dramatically. Millions of Christians, pastors and people in the workplace, are discovering that their vocation gives them a mission field were they can and must live out their calling. The most remarkable stories of kingdom advances are being reported where Christians in the workplace begin to grasp this and act on it. Graham is one of the forerunners of this stream of Christians in the marketplace. He demonstrates this in his business and daily life with great effect. I encourage you to read this book with a pen and paper in hand, listen to what the Holy Spirit says to you and 'go and do likewise.'

– Dr Bennie Mostert, Prayer Mobilizer (Jericho Walls International / 24/7)

People often ask, "What is my calling?". The answer is partly simple: the majority of us are called to the marketplace. The interwoven stories of Graham and Dion will encourage you to make your occupation your vocation, your job a 'beroep', in the true sense of the word. I highly commend these good friends to you; read their story so that your heart will be encouraged, your mind renewed, and your spirit emboldened. God, being a lawyer, understands legal precedent, so what he has done for them he can do for you and me if we walk in similar obedience. Make their story a springboard for your story. 'But, he is successful and if I had his money I could also serve God,' you may say. Don't ask for money like Graham – ask for humility like Graham. Don't ask for a ministry like Dion's, but minister with all that you have, right where you are. Don't wait for one great thing to do, but take the next step of obedience. I am delighted that Graham and Dion are challenging us to integrate our work and faith so that we can be a part of the extraordinary company of ordinary marketplace people who are extending the kingdom through daily business.

– Brett Johnson – President, The Institute for Innovation, Integration & Impact, Saratoga, California

'Take the Church to the people and the Gospel to the world'. This is the cry of our time as voiced by Graham Power and Dion Forster in this very practical book. Brave individuals, like Graham, are needed to make these new roads of Transformative Life into the Monday to Saturday world. This book will certainly develop a better Kingdom mindset in all who read it.

– Rev Cassie Carstens, Founder of three leadership training initiatives that have trained leaders from more than a hundred countries

Graham Power is a man whose personal experience transformed his life, the lives of his workers, the lives of his close associates and now the world. I admire him and continue to learn from his wisdom. Now with this book many will be empowered to accomplish all God has prepared for them.

– Al Caperna, CEO CMC Group; Director call2all business track

# CONTENTS

# ACKNOWLEDGEMENTS

## Graham Power

Accepting Jesus as my Lord and Savior in 1999 was the most important thing that I have ever done. In the years that have passed since that night where I knelt down in my study and gave Him my life, my family and my business – twenty-four hours a day, seven days a week – I have been more richly blessed than I could ever have imagined beforehand! This book shares some of that story. In truth, this whole book is an acknowledgement of Christ my King! It is because of his transforming power in my life that I have been privileged to experience so much, and play some part in the wonderful plan that He has for my / our companies, the industry in which we work and the nation in which we live. It is God who gave me the opportunities and the ability to achieve what I have – He deserves all the honour and the glory!

I am a businessman, so when Jesus saved me He dealt with that very important part of my life as well. It has been an incredibly rewarding, and sometimes even a challenging journey to live so openly and boldly for Christ – but I would not have it any other way!

There are many special friends who have supported me and journeyed with me as I've learnt how to live my whole life for Christ. First, I want to say how thankful I am to my wife Lauren. We recently celebrated our thirtieth wedding anniversary. She has been a loving and supportive companion since I first fell in love with her (as a fifteen-year-old schoolgirl) in high school. I am so grateful for her gentle and quiet nature – I thank God each day for the privilege of being loved and being able to love. Lauren and I have been blessed with three wonderful children, Gary, Nadene and Alaine. In recent years our family has grown as Gary married Ilene and Nadene married Stephen. Our grandchildren, Goerdie and Robert (and Nadene and Stephen's baby that will be born this year) are a reminder to me that I have a responsibility to work for a better, Christ-healed South Africa for my children and grandchildren. It is not easy to balance the demands of a growing company, a developing ministry and one's family. I am so thankful to God that all my children know and serve the Lord and that they share with me in this wonderful task of ministry in the marketplace.

Within the Power Group of companies there have been so many people who have helped us to grow and discover more about what it means to serve Jesus in the marketplace. You will read about many of them in the pages of this book. In truth, there are far too many special friends in the company who deserve to be mentioned, but because of the constraints of space and time we had to select just a few stories and testimonies to share. The Power Group of companies is an amazing 'family' of people – shaped by God for an incredible destiny. I want to express my sincerest thanks to our CEO, André du Preez, and the rest of our senior leadership team, for their willingness to be used by Christ to 'transform the lives of people in Africa through infrastructure development'. Moreover, I am grateful that they have been generous to release me from many of my duties I hold in the company in order to 'run' with the visions that God gave me for the Global Day of Prayer and Unashamedly Ethical. I am grateful for their unwavering commitment and dedication to the tasks that God has placed before us. While it is not without its challenges to be a Christian company radically committed to ethics, I can say that it is a joy and a blessing to be part of such a special team of dedicated people.

Finally, I want to thank Dawie and Isebel Spangenberg (who have played a leading role in the roll-out of the Global Day of Prayer), Etienne Piek (International co-ordinator of Global Day of Prayer) and Steve Johnstone (International co-ordinator of Unashamedly Ethical) and their teams for their ongoing commitment to mobilise the world for prayer, and challenge people across the globe to make the commitment to being 'Unashamedly Ethical'. I know that God longs to transform and renew the whole earth, and I have seen how God has used this special group of people to play a part in that. Please pray for them and for the staff of the Power Group of companies as God continues to unfold his plan among us.

My special thanks to Dion Forster, a close friend and confidant, who, having started out as my young minister at the Methodist Church in Somerset West (at the time of my conversion), now sits in the office alongside mine and assists with the work of the Global Day of Prayer, Unashamedly Ethical and various other ministry activities I am involved in. Dion has done the writing for this book, while I've contributed through telling the stories and sharing some experiences that you will read about in the pages that follow. I want to thank Dion for doing an amazing job! Thanks also to his wife Megan and their children, Courtney and Liam, whom Lauren and I regard as our extended grandchildren.

## Dion Forster

The Zulu people of Southern Africa have a saying: *'umuntu ngumuntu ngabantu'.* Roughly translated it means, 'we become more fully human through our relationships with others'. This book truly is a testimony to the fruit of such significant relationships.

First, I rejoice to acknowledge that without Christ I am nothing. Moreover, without Him this project could never have been done. He is not only the central focus of this book, He is the true author and the very reason why there is a story to share!

Then, I wish to honour my wife Megan and our children Courtney and Liam. They are an immeasurable gift from God. In our life together I find great joy, blessing and hope for the future. I am thankful for their extraordinary patience with me as I've tested the contents of these pages on them; slipping away late at night or early in the morning to write.

In this book you will read about one of the most remarkable men of our age, Graham Power. Graham is extraordinary because he has achieved so much in his life. He is a businessman second to none, a brave and devoted follower of Christ, and a wonderful friend and companion in ministry. However, what most sets him apart from his peers is his humility. I can say of Graham what Jesus said of Nathanael in John 1:47: He is someone 'in whom there is no guile'(The Amplified Bible). Graham has allowed me to participate in the adventure of a lifetime! My ministry has found a new passion and intensity since he has invited me to serve Christ in the market-place. I am truly thankful to him and all the staff of the Power Group of companies. Among them I am discovering what it means to be a faithful follower of Christ where it truly matters!

Then I wish to acknowledge the incredible work of the Global Day of Prayer and Unashamedly Ethical teams. As Graham has already mentioned, this small group of dedicated people are being used by God to transform the world through prayer and the revitalisation of ethics, values and clean living. Dawie Spangenberg, Etienne Piek, Steve Johnstone and their teams are a source of constant amazement and inspiration. I also want to thank my friend Rev Gareth Killeen, an expert on ministry in the market-place, for reading through the final text of the book. He not only helped to spot some basic errors, but also contributed numerous theological and practical insights.

Finally, I want to thank the team at Struik Christian Media: Fiona Lee, Elsabé Barlow, Lana Coetzee, and our editor, Trix Pauw. Their excitement throughout the writing of this book was contagious. I am also thankful for their extreme patience and their support! It is such a blessing to work with people whose passion it is to share the message of the Gospel in a manner that changes lives and inspires people.

# FOREWORD

God has been speaking eloquently and repeatedly to the church about his heart for, and his upcoming move in, the marketplace. Dr Billy Graham, one of the most respected leaders and surely the most perceptive modern evangelist, has stated that God's next move will be in the marketplace. His statement is consistent with the words spoken by the prophet Joel and quoted by Peter when he preached the first sermon of the Church Age in Acts 2. God's Spirit will be poured out on all people (see Acts 2:17, NIV), clearly implying that the end-time revival will happen in the marketplace since that is where most of 'all people' reside.

This book is co-authored by two of God's choicest gifts to the church and to the world – Graham Power and Dion Forster. It reflects 'what the Spirit is saying to the churches in this day and age'. Consequently, those who have ears are instructed to hear.

Many people have written on the subject of marketplace ministry and Dion and Graham are quick and gracious to acknowledge that they stand on the shoulders of early pioneers. But there are at least two important elements that make the content of this book unique: Firstly, it is the collaborative work of a pulpit and a marketplace minister who have and will continue to share in the trenches in God's kingdom. Their placement in those different, yet complementary arenas enables them to present God's message in well-balanced stereo. Secondly, it is the result of sound implementation of Biblical principles. It is not theoretical, but practical; fully sustained by experience that serves as an example for others to follow. Graham and Dion's stories are extraordinary, but they are rooted in ordinary, everyday situations, making the challenge and the instruction appealing and accessible to everyone.

As someone who has devoted his life to seeing transformation come to cities and nations, I welcome this book and highly and enthusiastically recommend it to anyone with a burden to see our world become a better place as God's will in heaven begins to be reflected on earth.

Ed Silvoso
*Author of* Anointed for Business *and*
Transformation: Change the Marketplace and You Change the World
*CEO of International Transformation Network*
*www.transformnourworld.org*

Miracles are a retelling in small letters of the very
same story that is written across the whole world in
letters too large for some of us to see.

– CS Lewis

'For I know the plans I have for you,' declares
the LORD, 'plans to prosper you and not to harm you, plans to give you hope and a future. Then you
will call upon me and come and pray to me, and I will listen to you. You will seek me and find me when
you seek me with all your heart. I will be found by you,' declares the LORD.

– Jeremiah 29:11–14b

'… [let] your Kingdom come, [let] your will be
done on earth as it is in heaven …'

– Matthew 6:10

# INTRODUCTION

## AN UNFOLDING STORY OF GRACE AND DISCOVERY

### A Mixture of Peace and Exhilaration

Long before I knew it, even before I was born, God had a dream for my life! In fact, God has a dream for your life too (see Psalm 139:13–18). From humble beginnings, through the years that were driven by personal aspiration, to the peace and fulfilment that I experience now, God has been unfolding a story! Each day is a new chapter filled with excitement, discovery and a greater realization of my purpose on earth. God is still writing the story of my life and for that I am eternally thankful.

Over the last half a century I have had the immeasurable privilege of experiencing many wonderful things. I have worked very hard to grow the Power Group of companies, one of South Africa's largest and most successful companies in the civil engineering and construction industry. I own many of the things I longed for as a younger man and have achieved many of the personal goals I set for myself. Yet, as Paul writes to the Philippians, 'I consider everything a loss compared to the surpassing greatness of knowing Christ Jesus my Lord' (Phil 3:8). Indeed, none of these achievements compares to the single most important discovery of my life – the discovery that I was made by God to use my life, my creativity, my energy and my abilities to partner with Him for eternal significance.

It has been an exhilarating journey of discovery and growth! I have come to understand a great deal about myself, my place in the world, and God's intention for me as I have carefully allowed Him to write new chapters in the story of my life.

Moreover, I have discovered a sense of peace that surpasses any possible financial reward or social accolade. I acknowledge that my story is only just starting. I still have so much to learn and I work each day to discipline myself to live more closely with God and more obediently within his will. However, I am so thankful for what I have experienced thus far that I want to share some of it with you.

My prayer is that you will also come to experience the mixture of peace and exhilaration that comes from living your life, your *whole life*, as God intended it to be lived!

## A Moment of Grace — Where the Story Begins

From a very early age I had a dream to rise from my humble beginnings to a position of social and economic prominence. I grew up as one of five children in a working-class home. My father was a motor mechanic and my mother pedalled her bicycle to work in a local store each day. Most of my clothes were 'hand downs' from my older siblings and my bike had numerous coats of paint on it, as it was given to each successive child. I did not have the luxury of a university education – so, when my father passed away and I had finished school I went straight to work for a local construction company.

Because of my drive for wealth and financial independence I worked harder, smarter and longer than most of my peers and quickly rose through the ranks of the company. By 1983 I realised that I could use the skill and knowledge I had acquired to start my own business. So with one employee, a small investment from a family member, a mortgage on my home and one small truck I started doing small paving jobs. That was the start of the Power Group of companies. Today the Power Group is one of the largest privately owned civil engineering and construction companies in Southern Africa, with its core business in highway construction and township development.

However, in spite of this success I soon came to realise that I longed for something more, something truly meaningful and significant, something that money and success could not provide.

*Lord, you have created us for yourself, and our hearts are restless until they find their rest in you.*

— ST AUGUSTINE

When you own the cars, the houses and the farms; and when the thrill of bigger and bigger business deals no longer holds the appeal it used to, you start asking some serious questions about life! I now know, of course, that like so many others I was simply trying to fill a spiritual void in my life with achievement and possessions. St Augustine said it so well when he wrote 'Lord, you have created us for yourself, and our hearts are restless until they find their rest in you.'

While all this was happening in my life God was busy crafting a testimony! Little did I know that there were a number of people praying for me (we will tell some of their stories later in this book).

One friend in particular, Mike Winfield, had invited me to an industry-related Christian breakfast a number of times. I had always turned him down – at that stage I believed quite firmly that faith had no place in one's work life. One's Christianity should be kept to that hour in church on a Sunday. However, Mike told me that a number of people from the construction industry, as well as some prominent city officials, would be attending this breakfast meeting and so I decided to go along (if for no other reason than to 'network' and build new contacts for business). God had other plans for me that morning.

Michael Cassidy was speaking and that day I heard the message of the Gospel with such clarity and authority as I had never heard it before. I left there challenged by the message that God loved me, that Jesus had died for me on the cross and that God had a divine purpose for my life! A few months later I was invited to a similar breakfast and this time the world-renowned cricketer, Peter Pollock, was speaking. I could identify with Peter; like me, he had sought his acclaim through his own ability and achievements. And, like me, even though he had achieved among the highest accolades in his field, he told of how that achievement was not enough, as for many years he had still searched for something more significant. I am sure you can see where this is going? Well, that morning as Peter told of how he had discovered peace and true life in Christ I was convinced that I needed to make a change in my own life. When Peter invited those gathered to say the 'sinner's prayer', I quietly repeated it after him. Then he asked that while all our eyes were closed and no-one was looking we should raise our hand if we had said the prayer. Well, I raised my hand and *someone was looking*, because the next day I received a phone call from a local Christian, Adolph Schultz. And so my journey with Jesus began! Adolph spent many hours with me in the subsequent months, helping me to understand the basics of the Christian faith and also to understand that God has a very special purpose and ministry for all Christians in the marketplace.

I can assure you that the journey since then has been the most remarkable, rewarding and transforming experience of my life! What has been most remarkable about it has been the discovery that God had been planning my life through experiences, lessons in business, relationships and network, and a host of other things, long before I even knew Him!

In the chapters of this book my friend and pastor, Dr Dion Forster, and I will share a number of insights and lessons we have learnt as we have grown on this journey of significance together. I shall share some of my experiences and Dion will share some of his. Dion will tell the stories of what God has done with us and through us and he will also share some pointers, scriptures, challenges and encouragement to help you along the way.

– *Graham Power*

## Turning Your Ordinary Day into an Extraordinary Calling

My journey with Graham Power began a short while before he came to know the Lord personally. In fact, I had had contact with his employees before I came to know him.

Graham occasionally worshipped at the church where I was a pastor – by his own admission he only came to church when there was pressure from his wife and no good sport on television! But, as Graham has already said, God had a plan to reach him where he wanted to use him – in the marketplace! There were a number of very committed and dedicated Christians working at the Power Group of companies and we are blessed that today there are many more! These faithful followers of Christ had started prayer and intercession groups for the company, their bosses and their colleagues. In fact, they even prayed for their customers, suppliers and other companies in their industry! And so they invited me to come and share with their Christian group at the company on a few occasions and through their faithfulness I caught the vision of praying for and getting alongside the business people in my congregation. Sadly, few pastors are trained to care for their flock outside of the ministries and activities of the church. But God was busy working in my life as well and so Graham was put at the top of my prayer list!

Needless to say, it has been one of the most remarkable, rewarding and blessed privileges to journey alongside Graham over the last decade and a bit. I have learnt so much about how God wants to use each and every person for ministry and particularly how God's priority for one of the least reached places in the world should shape our efforts to disciple and train Christians to fulfil their calling in the marketplace.

Most people will spend between sixty and seventy percent of their lives at work. Consider that the most productive part of your life (between the ages of twenty and sixty) will be spent working. Not only that, but the majority of us will also spend the largest part of our day, from when we open our eyes in the morning until we close them at night, engaged in work-related activities. This is an incredible investment of time, energy and creativity. When you think about it in this way you soon come to understand that God has a very particular desire for that huge portion of your life. What you do with your everyday life has eternal consequences. Note that I did not say it *could* have eternal consequences; I said that your work *has* eternal consequences. God cares about every part of your life, not just the parts that are spent in church and at church-related activities.

I am certain that when Jesus taught his disciples to pray '… [let] your Kingdom come, [let] your will be done on earth as it is in heaven' (Matt 6:10), He was not thinking only about what people would do in Church services on Sunday! You can be sure that Jesus was thinking about what his followers would do with every moment of their lives during the week, in every place where they lived their lives. Yes, Jesus was praying that his followers would live with Him and for Him every moment of every day of the week!

There are many millions of people who are missing one of the greatest windows of opportunity for serving Christ – the opportunity to serve Jesus in the marketplace.

> *Very few Christians have begun to understand the incredible redemptive potential and transformational opportunity that they unknowingly miss every day when they go to work.*

More than just finding personal fulfilment for the majority of your waking hours, a ministry in the marketplace also happens to be one of the most accessible and sizeable mission fields in the world! If you think about the company, industry or geographic area in which you work, how many significant Christian programmes can you think of that operate in your sphere of influence? Some of us may be able to list one or two small groups, or a minor outreach. However, what is certain is that very few Christians have begun to understand the incredible redemptive potential and transformational opportunity that they unknowingly miss every day when they go to work.

## The Unfolding Story of This Book ...

In the chapters of this book Graham and I share a number of the most important principles that we have learnt about ministry in the marketplace. While I have done most of the writing, Graham is the one who has contributed most in terms of insight and experience in what it takes to do marketplace ministry. Much of what we have discovered is available in greater technical detail in the books of our friends, such as Ed Silvoso, Os Hillman and John Maxwell.

Our intention is to offer some truly practical, sometimes challenging, hopefully inspiring insights into the tools and processes that you can use to transform your ordinary day into an extraordinary calling and by doing so, transform your workplace.

So, we would like to encourage you to embark on this journey with a great sense of expectation! Let the testimonies and lessons in this book serve you. Moreover, we want to assure you that this book was birthed in prayer. Both Graham and I have sought the Lord's guidance and inspiration in writing these pages and we have prayed for you and asked friends to do the same, as we have anticipated all the various people who will read the book.

Our greatest desire is to see you doing your very best to honour God as you are positioning yourself for an experience of God's miraculous power and blessing in your life and work! It may just be that, as He did for Graham, God wants to take you on a remarkable journey of exhilaration mixed with peace as you come to discover how you transform your ordinary workday into an extraordinary calling!

– *Dr Dion Forster*

Do not let your occupation block your destiny; instead, allow your destiny to shape your business by turning it into your ministry.

– Ed Silvoso

For we are God's workmanship, created in Christ Jesus to do good works, which God prepared in advance for us to do.

– Ephesians 2:10

# 1

## THE BIG QUESTION

## What Should I Spend the Rest of My Life Doing?

When you commit your life to the Lord, you will undoubtedly be challenged by what I call 'The Big Question'. How you answer this question will be a decision that can transform your life for ever.

Fairly soon after Graham committed his life, his family and his business to the Lord he also came up against this question: What Should I Spend the Rest of My Life Doing? This is a critical question and it probably is the most important question that anyone can ever ask! You see, the Bible tells us that God meticulously and carefully creates us for a purpose – you have a particular divine design that shapes your life's purpose and destiny. Paul tells the Christians in Ephesus that they are '… God's workmanship, created in Christ Jesus to do good works, which God prepared in advance for them to do' (Eph 2:10). The Greek word 'created' (*poiema*), which is used in this verse, refers to the process of carefully designing and constructing something for a very particular purpose. So few people realise that, because they were very carefully constructed for a purpose, they will never be able to fully honour their Creator, or find inner peace, until they do what they were designed for!

After Graham was saved his greatest desire was to honour God with his whole life. In the 1995 movie *Braveheart* William Wallace (played by Mel Gibson) says the following challenging line: 'Every man dies; not every man really *lives*.' Graham is the kind of person who gives his all! I soon came to realise that he really wanted to live for Jesus, but he was unsure of how to do that. And so, as many other business people have done over the years, he approached me, his pastor, for some guidance and insight.

---

*If I truly love Jesus and want to serve Him, does it mean that I must give up my job and become a pastor?*

---

We decided to take a two-day retreat at one of Graham's holiday homes at the Breede River to pray, talk and read the scriptures together. One night, as we sat next to the fire, I remember Graham asking me something like, 'If I truly love Jesus and want to serve Him, does it mean that I must give up my job and become a pastor?' He was seriously considering entering 'full-time ministry', and the only model he knew was the model that he saw in church on Sundays – pastoral ministry.

Well, as we prayed and talked it became abundantly clear that God was calling him into ministry! However, it also became clear that God was not calling him to become a pastor; rather He was calling him to a very different kind of ministry, one much better suited to his life's journey and his 'divine design'!

## A Businessman's Realization ...

The question: 'Should I become a pastor?' is a very common one for people who love Jesus sincerely. Most Christians' understanding of ministry is shaped by what they experience in church and see in the media. In these arenas pastors, priests and ministers are our most visible and active ministry role models. Just consider that the majority of sermons that we hear come from pastors. These dedicated and committed full-time church workers champion so much of the church's life and work, not to mention that most of us have come to respect our pastor's faith and knowledge of the Bible. The result of this is that many people assume that if you *really* love God and want to serve Him you must become a pastor of a church.

Of course it does not help that most of our churches reinforce this perception. If we were honest we would have to admit that there are very few churches that equip their members for ministry in their workplace; rather we encourage them to serve almost exclusively within the life of the local congregation. If you are a teacher the church will get you teaching Sunday school, if you are an accountant then surely you must be involved in running the church's finances …

The outcome of this perspective on ministry is that most Christians never even consider that their most significant ministry opportunity may be in the place where they spend most of their week – their workplace! Moreover, rather than you having to learn a completely new set of skills for ministry, God may just want to use what you already know, and already do well, to serve his kingdom. I often tell people that God does not waste experience!

For the majority of people who read this book the answer to the question, 'Should I become a pastor?' is probably, 'No'. It is far more likely that God wants to use your gifts, abilities, network of relationships and life's experience outside of your local congregation in the place where you work.

So, at the end of our two-day retreat Graham and I both knew that God had *designed* him for a truly significant ministry that would reach far beyond the walls of our local church. But like most good things it took some work to figure out what that meant.

## Onto the Pulpit or Into the World? A Pastor's Confession ...

When Graham turned to me for guidance and insight while wrestling with 'The Big Question' in his life, something else happened. Without Graham realising it at the time, just by asking this question and turning to me for guidance, the Lord had already started to use him to start a process of change within me that would transform my ministry as well. Graham's quest became a catalyst that would take me on a new path.

Let me ask you a question – what would you do if the most successful businessman in your city were saved and was a member of your church? I've asked many pastors and church leaders this question over the years and the answers they gave are surprisingly similar! Most of them have said something along the lines of, 'Dion, you should use his gifts within the ministry of your church to grow the church!'

On that wonderful Sunday morning in 1999 when Graham came to speak to me after a service and told me, 'Dion, I've given my life to Jesus! What does God want me to do?' I faced one of the greatest temptations I had ever faced in my ministry! You see, every pastor longs to grow a strong, faithful and effective church! My desire was no different. We were in the midst of an incredible growth phase in our congregation's life! Because of some new real estate development in our area many families were moving into our neighbourhood and our church was abuzz with activity! Our programmes, our staff and our membership were growing at a rapid rate. In fact, our main service was getting so full that we had to carry in extra chairs and put people in the adjacent halls just to fit them all into worship! If the truth be told, I was a little out of my depth, I didn't quite know how to manage the increasing demands associated with our church's growth. It was in this situation that Graham asked me 'What does God want me to do?' Wow, what a temptation!

I went home that morning and said to my wife, Megan, 'God has answered our prayers! He has saved Graham! I'm going to invite him to serve on our leadership team and our finance committee!' Just think about it – Graham had been blessed with an incredible acumen for growing organisations. His companies, the Power Group of companies, were among the fastest growing companies in their industry. He is wealthy, successful and an incredible leader. Not only could he help us to grow our church, but he could probably help us to raise the necessary finances we needed to expand our buildings and staff.

Thankfully, God did not allow that to happen! I soon realised that if I had brought Graham onto my leadership team he may have tried his best to add value for a few months, but he would eventually have moved on, perhaps even feeling frustrated and unfulfilled.

*While God intended every Christian to be a minister, God never intended every Christian to be a pastor!*

You see, like most Christians, Graham was not designed for church leadership, he was actually designed for another type of ministry – ministry in the marketplace.

It is on this very point that the church, and Christians, often go wrong – in our sincere desire to honour God and put gifted people to use in ministry, we allow the good to trip up the great. The simple truth is that while God intended every Christian to be a minister, God never intended every Christian to be a pastor!

And so, I thank God that He directed Graham to follow his true calling, to live according to his design and to have the courage and commitment to work out what it means to serve Jesus according to his unique design (see Ephesians 2:10). Graham had acquired years of experience in the marketplace, he had a significant network of relationships and his abilities, his passion and his gifts were all designed so that God could use him in his company and his industry (see 1 Corinthians 12:7–10).

When you operate according to your design God can truly use you!

*Just like every great designer, inventor and engineer, God rejoices to see his creation doing what He planned it to do!*

There is always a wonderful consequence to being obedient to God's call and fitting in with God's 'divine design' for your life. When Graham started living his whole life, including his business life, as an obedient act of worship to God some remarkable miracles began to take place! Moreover, there are some personal rewards; the first reward is the peace of knowing that he is learning to do obediently what God had intended for his life. The second great reward is seeing how God uses the aspects of his 'divine design' to transform his life and the lives of others. In a later section of this book we will tell you how Graham's business has become his ministry and share some of the wonderful testimonies of how God has used him and his company to bring about amazing transformations in the marketplace.

Just like every great designer, inventor and engineer, God rejoices to see his creation doing what He planned it to do! God wants to invest even more of his creative love and power in your life. All that you need to do is work out what God made you for. Then start doing that with passion, commitment and intention, and watch how God does the rest!

Remember that you were carefully and deliberately designed and created to be used by God for ministry – it is very likely that God wants to work in you and through you where you spend most of your day!

## Points to Ponder

- You have a 'divine design' (see Ephesians 2:10). Do you know what your 'divine design' is? If you do not know what your 'divine design' is, please take some time to pray about and discover the following:
  - » *Spiritual Gifts* (see 1 Cor 12:7–10). The nine spiritual gifts (also called the charismatic gifts) listed in 1 Corinthians 12 are wisdom, knowledge, discerning of spirits (human, angelic, demonic), speaking in tongues, interpretation of tongues, prophecy, faith, working of miracles and healing. For example, the Lord has blessed Graham with the gift of leadership. This means that he can rely on God to use him to lead people and systems in his work life, sometimes stretching himself a little beyond his own ability, because he knows that through this spiritual gift God will use him to bring about transformation and blessing!
  - » *Your Passions.* When God created you He gave you certain preferences. Some people long for a challenge, while others have a passion to bring calm and peace. Some people love business, while others are energised by sports. The things that you are passionate about give you energy. God wants to harness that energy and passion for his kingdom. What are you passionate about?

» *Your Unique Abilities.* There are some things that you can do uniquely well, better than anyone else. Graham has a wonderful capacity to do business well. He can see opportunities; he has the courage and appetite for risk to take things on that others would shy away from. Because he understands his abilities and has given them over to God, they become useful tools in God's kingdom. Just think about this – it was Graham's ability to take risks and his acquired skill to organise people and systems that allowed him to call the Christians of Cape Town together for the first Global Day of Prayer event at Newlands Rugby stadium in 2001 (on that day 45 000 Christians gathered for a day of repentance and prayer – now every country on earth participates in the Global Day of Prayer, an estimated 350 million people). God wants to use your unique abilities for the sake of his kingdom.

» *Your Unique Personality Type.* What kind of person are you? Are you an extrovert or an introvert? Do you love people? Do you love cities or the great outdoors? Your personality is a gift from God. It will shape who you are and what God wants you to do.

» *Life's Experience.* This is a very interesting one – Graham frequently tells how growing up in humble circumstances gave him the desire and drive for success in business. When he was saved he could turn that into a gift for God by making the move from success to significance! Frequently our best and worst life experiences make us uniquely qualified to be used by God. The loss of a loved one gives you tremendous empathy for others in that situation. The struggle of losing a business helps you offer comfort and hope to people who are facing that situation. If you look at your unique design, how have you been moulded and shaped by what you've been through? Remember that God can, and wants to use your life's experience to minister to others!

• You will never give your Creator glory, or find personal peace, until you do what you were created for. The most important question you can ask as a Christian is, 'What does God want me to do with the rest of my life?' How and where can you use your 'divine design' to bring God glory and find personal fulfilment? Like Graham, it is fairly likely that God will want to use you where you are. God never wastes precious relationships or developed skills and always remember that God has a perfect will and desire for every person and every place on earth (even the people you work with). So, what does God want you to do with the rest of your life?

- When you come to realise that you are already gifted, qualified and uniquely placed for ministry your life can be transformed! Moreover, when you start living out your 'divine design' the lives of those around you will also be touched and transformed. Make the choice today to discover how to spend the rest of your life doing what God designed you to do.

## Questions for Group Discussion

- Can you list your three primary spiritual gifts in order of importance? If you are not able to do so, it is important that you commit to discovering and developing your spiritual gifts. The use of these gifts will shape your destiny.
- Please read Ephesians 2:10. If you are in a group setting take some time to reflect upon the gifts, abilities, and purpose the *other* members of the group may have. Sometimes you can see something about a person that they may not be able to see about themselves. Try to find one unique purpose for which God has created each member of your group. Share this purpose with them and commit to pray for them as they seek to develop this purpose.
- If you were given enough money to survive comfortably, what would you choose to do with your life in order to honour God and find personal fulfilment? Is there any way that you can plan to work towards fulfilling that passion?
- Please read Psalm 90:12. Your life is a precious gift. You only have one life to live. What changes do you need to make in order to honour God with what remains of your life?
- Please pray for one another, asking God to give you wisdom to choose how best to spend the remainder of your life in order to honour God, bless others, and find personal peace.

Most Christians who on Sundays worship God to the tune of inspiring music fail to see that what they do during the week is also meant by God to be worship.

– Ed Silvoso

Whatever you do, work at it with all your heart, as working for the Lord, not for men, since you know that you will receive an inheritance from the Lord as a reward.

– Colossians 3:23–24

# 2

## WHY SHOULD I TAKE JESUS TO WORK?

### It is Time to Rethink Your Answer

ecently I was speaking to a friend about his work. I could see that he was frustrated and worn out and I had been trying to encourage him to see how God could use him just where he was. Somewhere along the line of our conversation he said, 'I live for the weekend! I dread going to work on Monday and when I'm at work I count the hours until Friday. If I didn't need the money I would have stopped working.' As I was driving back to my office later that morning, I thought, 'How sad that he is wishing away most of his life! Surely there must be something more meaningful to your work life than just hanging in there for a pay cheque!'

---

*Surely there must be something more meaningful to your work life than just hanging in there for a pay cheque!*

---

I'm sure that there are many people who live for the weekend and many more who simply work because they need the money! The good news is that you don't have to wish most of your life away. God has a wonderful plan to make what you do from Monday to Friday one of the most fulfilling and exhilarating parts of your week.

### All you Need is a Different Perspective ...

Over the years Graham and I have spoken to many deeply-committed Christians who have never considered that God may actually have something for them to achieve between Monday and Friday. We tend to place our lives into two boxes, a sacred box (everything we do for God), and a secular box (everything else we do). Very often business people think of their 'God stuff' as worship – and worship only happens in certain places (like church buildings) at certain times (like on a Sunday, or on Christmas and Easter). Everything else is simply 'my stuff' and it has very little to do with my worship. So, my work, my friendships, my community relationships, my sport – all of these 'other things' are outside of the sacred. The reality is that everything that we have, all that we are, and all that we do should be done for God.

---

*The reality is that everything that we have, all that we are, and all that we do should be done for God.*

---

From God's perspective there is no separation between work and worship. I once heard someone explain it in this way – imagine that you have a 'big worship switch' on your back. Each time that you enter into worship the switch is flicked on. Do think that God is honoured when your 'worship switch' is flicked off? Surely we should never stop worshipping God – even at work.

God has a perfect will for every person, for every situation and every place. When you begin to look at your workplace and the people that you work with from God's perspective you can see that He may just have an incredible mission for you to perform right where you are from Monday to Friday.

Paul instructed the Christians in the Colossian church saying, 'Whatever you do, work at it with all your heart, as working for the Lord, not for men, since you know that you will receive an inheritance from the Lord as a reward' (Col 3:23–24).

## Work as Worship

One of the first lessons that we need to learn is what Christian worship truly means. True Christian worship is so much more than just singing songs and praying with other Christians in church on Sunday. The word 'worship' comes from an old English word 'worth-ship', which had the meaning of recognising or ascribing worth to someone or something i.e., a person of Godly wisdom and authority may be worthy of respect. When we worship we are acknowledging that God is worthy of special attention, obedience and of our sacrifice and love. Worship can of course be something as wonderful as a heartfelt prayer of adoration or song of praise, but it can also be as simple as making a choice in favour of God's will over your own. When you are faced with a choice between doing something in accordance with God's loving will, or choosing your own will, it is an opportunity for worship. If you choose to do what God wants you to do you are declaring that God's will is worth more than your will – that is worship.

This is what Paul was saying when he wrote, 'Therefore, I urge you, brothers, in view of God's mercy, to *offer your bodies* as living sacrifices, holy and pleasing to God – *this is your spiritual act of worship*' (Rom 12:1). You can worship God with every choice you make, in every relationship you engage in, in every meeting, with every client – in short, you can use every moment of every day to worship God!

---

*If Jesus had your job, how do you think He would approach the tasks and the people you encounter every day?*

---

You can be certain that God wants to bless the people that you work with. He also has a perfect will for the business within which you work. Maybe God wants to use you to influence the values of your employer, or to lovingly transform the business practises of your industry. If Jesus had your job, how do you think He would approach the tasks and the people you encounter every day?

## The Courage to Take Responsibility!

Graham felt a strong sense of calling to begin to challenge business people to worship God through their business lives by committing themselves to Godly values, ethics and clean living. (You can read more about this challenge in the final chapter of this book.) It was as clear as daylight! God is not pleased by dishonest gain. Proverbs 11:1 says, 'The Lord abhors dishonest scales, but accurate weights are his delight.' So, Graham started by getting his own house in order – the domain over which God had given him authority had to become 'unashamedly ethical'. One morning in 1999 he called together all of the directors of the Power Group and informed them that they had to find and root out all dishonest practises in the company – naturally some of them were concerned. They asked how the company would be able to compete, and how they would win contracts. Over the last ten years God has shown how his ways are more worthy than corrupt ways! The Power Group has not only continued to do business according to Godly values and ethical practises, they have grown in these tough economic times.

## Marketplace Missionaries

Graham had realised that by 'taking Jesus to work' with him, he had transformed Monday to Friday into an act of sustained worship – the worship switch stayed on. Moreover, his work life had suddenly taken on a whole new meaning. As he sought

God's guidance, direction and help to impact people and systems with the Gospel, he was partnering God in mission.

Of course the great news is that God has promised to empower us and to remain with us always – we will never be forsaken or left alone when we are doing his will (Matthew 28:20). When you see the marketplace as a mission field into which God is sending you, everything changes. Meetings become an opportunity to share blessings and bring God's will to bear. Co-workers and clients are the people that God is sending you to love and serve. Every obstacle and challenge becomes an opportunity for God to show his power and grace – creating testimonies out of trials.

Points to Ponder

I encourage Christians to do a few simple things in order to take Jesus to work with them.

- *Acknowledge* that God wants to be worshipped every moment of every day (that includes Monday to Friday).
- *Commit* your work life to God in prayer. Just like a pastor would pray to the Lord asking for wisdom, guidance and insight to minister to his or her congregation, you should pray about your workplace and the people you encounter in your work life. Ask God to show you what He wants you to achieve and do during those precious hours when you are at work.
- *Take responsibility* for the favour and influence that God has given you and use every opportunity to bring God's will to bear on your sphere of influence. Whether you are a business owner, a manager, or someone who works directly with customers, makes little difference to God! Remember that Paul said, 'Whatever you do, work at it with all your heart, as working for the Lord …' (Col 3:23). God has used people in humble positions in our company to achieve some of the most amazing breakthroughs for his kingdom!
- *Be intentional* about including Jesus in your work life. You can start by asking a few basic questions:
  » If Jesus were doing my work, how would He do it differently?
  » If Jesus were working among the people that I come into contact with, how would He treat them?
  » If Jesus had faced the challenges that I face in my workplace, how would He have dealt with them?

- *Be practical* in making Jesus' presence felt in your workplace and through your work life. I follow a simple little discipline at the start of each week. On a Sunday evening after my children are asleep I take my appointment book and look through all of the meetings, tasks and to-do items that I will have to deal with. I go through each day slowly and I pray about the people, decisions and challenges and ask God to give me guidance, wisdom, insight and love to face them as Jesus would. It is amazing what a difference this little spiritual discipline makes to my week! God lovingly prepares me to face difficult people with grace. He frequently shows me solutions to complex problems and often instructs me to do a simple little thing in order to show his love to someone that I will meet during the week (whether it is blessing them with a little card, or buying them a book to read, or simply offering them some praise or encouragement for work well done).

How can you transform your work life into worship? What can you do to make Jesus' presence visible and real in your decisions and relationships from Monday to Friday? Remember that God deserves to be worshipped every moment of every day and you have an opportunity to ascribe great worth to Him for much more than just one hour on a Sunday!

Questions for Group Discussion
- Please read Colossians 3:23–24.
- What is God's attitude to work and labour?
- If Jesus had your job, working among the people you work with, doing the things you do during your workday, what do you think He would want to achieve? How different is that from what you are striving for?
- Give some practical and creative examples of how you can use your talents, abilities, attitude and effort to honour Jesus in your work life.
- Is there any particularly challenging element of your work life for which you need prayer? Please pray for one another and invite Jesus to help each of the members of your group to do their work as an act of worship. Also, please invite Jesus to work in you and through you to begin to bless the people you work with and transform the structures you work in each day.

Transformation doesn't happen in a vacuum. It is brought about by people who have
tapped into a well of resolve and a sense of purpose deep and powerful enough to enable
them to overcome the ominous and menacing challenges that stand at its gates
like intimidating guardians.

– Ed Silvoso

Therefore go and make <u>disciples</u> of all nations,
baptising them in the name of the Father and of the Son and
of the Holy Spirit and teaching them to obey everything I
have commanded you. And surely I am with
you always, to the very end of the age.

– Matthew 28:19–20

# 3

## BIG PLAN! BIG PURPOSE!
## Expect Great Things!

A few years ago I took my daughter to the circus. She loved the clowns and the animals! When the show was over we walked through the animal enclosure to see the star of the show – a fully grown, male African elephant. He is an impressive beast, massive, powerful, and thankfully very well trained. During the early part of the day, when there are no visitors to the showgrounds, the elephant is allowed to wander freely to exercise and graze. However, when the children and their parents arrive for the shows the large elephant is chained to a long chain in order to avoid any unforeseen incidents. I was amazed at how thin the chain was for such a large animal. I was certain that the elephant could easily break free from the chain if he exerted just a little pressure on it, but he did not. He would wander to the full length of the chain and when he felt it pulling on his leg, he would move back. Clearly the elephant had no intention of breaking the chain.

That evening when I got home I did a search on the internet and found that this behaviour is common in circus elephants – it is known either as 'circus elephant syndrome' or 'baby elephant syndrome'. When a baby elephant is being trained for a life in the circus it is chained or tied to a tree at night using either a thin chain or a rope. This is to stop the elephant from wandering away from the camp while the trainer is sleeping. The little elephant will pull and tug against its restraint with all its might! No matter how hard it tries, it simply cannot break the chain. And so it eventually comes to believe that the chain is unbreakable. One commentator said that years later when the elephant was much stronger and larger and certainly able to break the physical restraint that bound it, it was not the chain around its leg that held the elephant captive, but the chain in its mind.

Many of us struggle with a similar problem – because of disappointments, or through bad experiences and failed attempts, we have given up expecting great miracles for the hours we spend in our workplace! Some of us have simply never considered the possibilities that God has in store for us during an ordinary workday. Like the elephant, the obstacle to true freedom and life may simply require a change of heart and mind.

If more Christians were willing to see their lives from God's perspective, they would soon discover that God has big plans and a big purpose for them to achieve.

---

*If more Christians were willing to see their lives from God's perspective, they would soon discover that God has big plans and a big purpose for them to achieve.*

---

What you need is a God-inspired vision for work as mission and ministry that will allow you to see beyond the pressing tasks, the familiar people and the limitations of time and resources, in order to achieve what God wants for you and from you.

In this chapter I will present and discuss five paradigms, or shifts in mindset, that have shaped and informed our view of work as mission and ministry. These five paradigms are discussed in far greater detail and depth in Ed Silvoso's books *Anointed for Business* (Regal Books, 2002) and *Transformation: Change the Marketplace and You Change the World* (Regal Books, 2007). These five mindset changes have radically transformed not only our view of what it means to be a Christian in the workplace, but also the very purpose and reason why God calls us to engage in labour.

Paul admonishes the Christians in Rome to '... be transformed by the renewing of your mind. Then you will be able to test and approve what God's will is – his good, pleasing and perfect will' (Rom 12:2). I would encourage you to read this chapter more than once, allowing these paradigms to challenge your thinking about work and your role as a Christian in the workplace.

Each of the paradigms discussed below will be considered in greater detail in the other chapters of this book. In those chapters you will also find some practical suggestions and encouragements to help you make the shift from small plans and little purpose for your work life, to big plans and a big purpose!

# Be Transformed by the Renewing of Your Mind

## Paradigm 1: Discipleship is about more than just Individual people

In Matthew 28:18–20 Jesus says, 'All authority in heaven and on earth has been given to me. Therefore go and make disciples of all nations, baptising them in the name of the Father and of the Son and of the Holy Spirit, and teaching them to obey everything I have commanded you. And surely I am with you always, to the very end of the age'.

This command for Christians to 'go' into all the world has a number of implications for your ordinary workday. Firstly, when Jesus sends you into 'all the world' (Luke 16:15, NKJV) He is certainly thinking of the place where you work, not just the place where you worship! As we have already discussed, the *location* for your ministry is most likely where you already spend most of your time and energy – your workplace. Secondly, this passage not only outlines the location of your ministry, it also tells you what kind of ministry you should undertake in your workplace; *'make disciples of all nations.'* As a Christian you have the responsibility of discipling people into following the person and the ways of Jesus Christ. But note that the verse says that you are instructed to make disciples of 'all nations'.

Most Christians, and even most churches, miss these two crucial points – namely that Jesus is sending us into 'all the world' (even our workplaces) in order to 'disciple all nations'. In the many years that I served as pastor of a church I did a lot of work to try and reach individual people through the saving love of Jesus Christ. I preached, developed outreach projects and did everything that I could to share the 'good news' of Jesus' forgiving love for people. However, like many other pastors and churches I did very little to address the systems of sin in which the people around me live and work every day! Every day when you go to work you are faced with systems and structures that do not honour God. Unethical choices, immoral business dealings, ungodly greed, unloving treatment of workers – these are all things that grieve God's heart and destroy people's lives. Not only that, but how many of us work at companies that do not care for God's creation, are abusing the earth's resources and polluting the earth? The fruit of our labour, our taxes, may be supporting unjust and ungodly laws.

Each day when you go to work you have an opportunity to 'go into all the world' without having to go across the world. And while you are at work you have the responsibility of engaging both people and systems with the transforming and saving love of Jesus.

---

*Each day when you go to work you have an opportunity to 'go into all the world' without having to go across the world.*

---

When you take a stand about a matter of justice, or when you refuse to be part of an unethical deal, you are engaged in a mission – the mission of establishing God's kingdom where you work. When you use your gifts, talents and abilities to do good work, to contribute toward the good of society and the good of those with whom you work, you are engaged in ministry – the ministry of doing what Jesus would have done if He had your job.

The first mindset change you need to ask God to help you with is that of where you are called to be in ministry, and what you are called to do there. For Graham the message was clear! God had called Graham, as the owner of the Power Group of companies, to use his skill, influence and ability to transform the Power Group of companies, and through this to have an impact on the construction industry, and ultimately the nation.

## Paradigm 2: Wealth and Work have been Redeemed and so they must be Reclaimed for Christ's Glory and Honor

In Colossians 1:19–20 Paul says the following, 'For God was pleased to have all his fullness dwell in him [Jesus], and through him to reconcile to himself *all things*, whether things on earth or things in heaven.' I have read this passage so often, but I have never noticed those two little words, 'all things'. Jesus Himself says, 'For the Son of man is come to seek and to save that which was lost' (Luke 19:10, KJV).

What these two passages make clear is that when Jesus died for our salvation, he died not only to save people from the destruction of their sin; Jesus also died to redeem the rest of creation from the destruction of sin (including work, industry, politics, health, education, wealth and every existing thing). The word 'redeem' means to recover ownership of something by paying the price for it. For example, if you park your car in a parking garage, you first have to pay the price for the parking before your car can be released. Once you have paid for the parking and redeemed your ticket, you are free to leave the parking garage.

When Jesus died He not only paid the price for sins (those things that we do) but

He also paid the price for sin (the corruption and brokenness that exists in all creation). The incredible miracle of grace is that God trusts you and me enough to allow us to reclaim what Jesus has already redeemed.

---

*The incredible miracle of grace is that God trusts you and me enough to allow us to reclaim what Jesus has already redeemed.*

---

I explain this principle using the following explanation: People often ask me when I 'was saved'. They usually want to know the date on which I accepted salvation from my sins, which happened in 1986. However, I tell them that I was saved 2000 years ago when Jesus died for my sin and overcame it by rising from the dead! Jesus paid the price for my sin 2000 years ago, so that was when He saved me. I only *claimed* that salvation in 1986. He redeemed me, and I had the privilege of reclaiming the life that He had already redeemed.

Remember that Jesus died not just to save the souls of people, rather He died to save all of creation from the destruction of sin. Jesus paid the price so that the economic system of your country could be redeemed. Jesus paid the price so that the justice system of your country could be redeemed. Jesus paid the price so that every aspect of your world, including your work, could be redeemed.

So, each day when we go to work we have the privilege of reclaiming what Jesus has already paid the price for. It takes courage and wisdom to claim places, people and systems for Jesus. In the Power Group we have come to realise the importance of this task. Consider this, if there is a contract to build a new road and someone who does not serve Christ, or honour his ways, wins that contract, the road is not claimed for Jesus. Moreover, the wealth that is generated from that project may be used for evil, such as drugs, greed or corruption, rather than for good. So, we understand that we have a responsibility to work hard, to work well and to win the trust of our clients in order to do more and more work for the sake of establishing Christ's kingdom.

God wants you to do the same with your gifts, abilities, influence and work. You have opportunities each day, some great and some small, to reclaim people, places and systems for Jesus. This is why it is important for Christians to occupy leadership positions in their workplaces and communities. We need parents who serve Christ on our school boards to claim and influence educational institutions. We need Christians serving in political parties and organisations in order to claim these institutions and their decisions for Christ by influencing them with Godly principles and values.

Jesus died to redeem everything; through your work you can reclaim what Christ has redeemed.

## Paradigm 3: Every Christian is a Minister, and Work, when done for Christ and his Purposes, can be an Act of Worship

Have you ever thought of yourself as a 'full-time minister'? A lot of people have asked me how much time Graham spends on 'ministry' activities. When I ask them what they mean by that question a few have clarified that they want to know how much time Graham devotes to 'work' as the Chairman of the Power Group of companies, and how much time he devotes to ministry activities such as the Global Day of Prayer and Unashamedly Ethical campaigns.

My answer to the question 'How much time does Graham spend on ministry activities?' is a hundred percent! You see, Graham has understood what Paul wrote in Colossians 3:23–24, 'Whatever you do, work at it with all your heart, as working for the Lord, not for men, since you know that you will receive an inheritance from the Lord as a reward. It is the Lord Christ you are serving'. Note that Paul does not say that we can only use what we do in church, or for our church as ministry! He says 'whatever you do' work at it as if you are 'working for the Lord'. So, whether Graham is making decisions about housing projects, or mobilising people for prayer, it is all ministry because it is all done for Jesus.

When you do all your work for Jesus you are not only engaged in ministry that transforms the people and the systems you work among, you are also engaged in worship! Simply stated, worship is the act of acknowledging and ascribing worth to God and God's will. So, when you choose to work as if you are working for the Lord – making loving decisions, witnessing to Jesus' love and will in your speech, your actions and your choices – then you are ascribing worth to Jesus and his ways. This is worship.

Imagine for a moment that you were fitted with a 'worship switch' that you flicked on every time you entered into worship, and that flicked off every time you stopped worshipping. I am sure you would agree that the switch is flicked on when you are in a worship service. But, do you think that God is pleased when your worship switch is flicked off on a Monday morning as you go to work? No! God deserves to be worshipped with all that we are and all that we do.

When you think about your life in this way, your church worship service on a Sunday is just the beginning of worship; every moment of every day throughout the week can be worship 'with all your heart, as working for the Lord' since it is 'Christ you are serving' (Col 3:23–24).

So, I want to encourage you to start seeing the tasks of your day, the place where you work and the people that you encounter differently. Each one of these presents you with an opportunity for ministry and worship. Flick on that worship switch and keep it on all day, all week.

## Paradigm 4: We are to take the Good News of Jesus to the Places of Darkness and He will build His Church there

Matthew records a remarkable conversation between Jesus and Peter in Matthew 16:13–20. There is one particular part of that conversation that stands out for me because it has given me a remarkable new perspective on the purpose and location of the church; the statement is found in Matthew 16:18 where Jesus says, '... on this rock I will build my church, and the gates of Hades will not overcome it'.

There are two critical mind shifts that we are encouraged to make in this verse. Firstly, Jesus is clear that He is the one who builds the church! Our task is not to engage primarily in building the membership numbers of our churches. When we come to realise that our task is simply to be obedient to his will, to seek to love people and act as agents of transformation where He directs us, then He will build his church. Secondly we learn from this verse that the place where God wants to build his church most is at the gates of Hell. Where it is darkest we are called to be light! Where the world is facing its greatest decay we are called to be salt that preserves (Matt 5:13–16). Many of us have made the mistake of thinking that we need only bring darkness to the light in order to honour God – by inviting friends, family and colleagues to church services and church events. This is a good start, but if you truly want to see the power of God in operation you should take light into dark places.

Where would you find darkness within your workweek? I am certain that there are some people and places that could do with a little salt and light where you work! When you start being a minister – salt and light – in the marketplace, you'll be surprised at how quickly Jesus establishes his church there!

So, at the Power group we have taken the bold step of inviting Christians to gather for prayer and teaching during their lunch hour, or before their workday starts. We encourage them to love people into the presence of God through their actions and words – we have many Christians whom Jesus is building into the church right where they work each day. It is a source of great blessing to all of us and to God!

## Paradigm 5: True Transformation must be Tangible and Visible

Did you know that Jesus had a 'mission statement' for his ministry on earth? You can read it in Luke 4:16–21. It is interesting to see that all the things that Jesus came to do were practical, tangible expressions of God's love for the world. I have heard so many sermons on this passage that I sometimes forget just how practical Jesus intended his ministry to be. When Jesus said He had come to bring 'good news to the poor' (Luke 4:18) what do you think He meant? Let us approach it from a slightly different perspective: what is good news for a poor person? I have been in need a few times in my life, and I can tell you when you are poor good news is not a sermon! It is good news when you have food and money to pay your bills, it is great news when you get a job that pays you a salary with which you can support your family and yourself.

One of the big failings of the contemporary church, and that means you and me, is that we do not always bless the people around us in tangible and visible ways. When someone is ill we say things like, 'I'll pray for you' – while this is an expression of care, I can assure you that the person would feel so special and loved if you took them a meal! I know that God longs for Christians to get practical and creative about making the 'good news' real for the people around them. We should not be asking 'what does the good news sound like?' Rather, we should ask 'what does the good news feel like, and what does good news look like?' This is Jesus' way!

---

*God longs for Christians to get practical and creative about making the 'good news' real for the people …*
*We should not be asking 'what does the good news sound like?',*
*rather we should ask 'what does the good news feel like, and what does good news look like?'*

---

As you think about the people among whom you work, what would be truly good news for them? Is there a single mother who is battling to make ends meet? Perhaps you have a co-worker who is struggling to cope with his workload, or maybe someone whose child is ill – what could you do to make the 'good news' visible and tangible for these people?

Sometimes it is the simplest things, like a phone call, or a visit, that make people feel loved and cared for. At other times you will need to be a little more creative and sacrificial in what you do.

I have a simple little discipline that I learnt from Dr Bruce Wilkinson in his book *'You Were Born for This'* (Multnomah Books, 2009). At the start of each month I take a small sum of money and put it into a particular pocket in my pants – this is my 'God Pocket'. I do not use that money for anything other than what God wants me to do with it. I do not use it to buy something to drink when I am thirsty, or to pay for parking when I have left my wallet in the car. This is God's money. Recently my wife and I were at a restaurant celebrating a birthday when we struck up a conversation with our waitress. She told us that she is a single mother who has three children. Her twins were celebrating their eighth birthday the following day. As she walked away I felt God nudging me to give her the money from my 'God pocket'. So, after we had settled the bill and given her a tip I gave her the money and said, 'This money was given to me by a friend. He told me to give it to someone to show them that they are special and loved. My friend would want me to give this money to you as a gift for your children'. She was so overjoyed by the gift! Megan and I knew that we had done the right thing. The witness that we had shared with this woman throughout the evening was powerfully enforced by this simple act of generosity.

How practical is your love for the people around you? You can achieve so much more through a few simple, loving acts than you can through hundreds of eloquent sermons.

*Preaching the good news without love is like giving someone a good kiss when you have bad breath. No matter how good your kiss, all the recipient will remember is your bad breath.*

— ED SILVOSO

## Points to Ponder

Romans 12:2 says that you must 'be transformed by the renewing of your mind. Then you will be able to test and approve what God's will is – his good, pleasing and perfect will'. It may be that God wants to transform your work life by giving you a new perspective on ministry in the marketplace.

Please take some time to pray and consider the following questions:

- Do you know what God's 'good, pleasing and perfect will' is for the place and people where you work? If your answer is 'no', then please pray and ask God to reveal his will to you as you read the rest of this book, as you go to work and as you pray and read the scriptures.
- Please take some time to review the headings of each of the five paradigms discussed in this chapter. To which of these five mindsets do you need to make a change in order to honour God in your workplace?
- Is there anyone with whom you can share what you have learnt about ministry in the marketplace from this chapter? Research has shown that we learn better when we share our knowledge with others. Moreover, you may just find a Christian co-worker who also longs for greater significance and blessing as you share these five points with him or her.

In conclusion, remember that God cares just as much about what you do, as God cares about who you are.

## Questions for Group Discussion

- We read in Matthew 28:18–20 that Jesus' desire is to use Christians, like you, to transform nations. Share with each of the members of the group what it means for your work life to be 'discipled' for Jesus.
- In what ways could your work life contribute towards the discipling of your nation? What would you need to do, or commit to do, in order to start discipling your work life?
- Are there any people, systems or places within your sphere of influence that have not yet been reclaimed for Christ? What would it take to reclaim these elements? What can you commit yourself to do in order to do so?
- Every Christian is a minister – what makes ministry different from 'just working'? What do you need to start doing for your work life, and in your work life, in order to live as a minister?

- What is the most significant and visible need among the people within your context? Remember, transformation must be tangible and visible. How would you begin to address and resolve some of the most pressing 'felt needs' among the people in your sphere of influence?
- Please take some time in prayer to commit each member of your group to God's 'big plan' and 'big purpose' for their lives.
- It will be important to keep a record of the commitments you are making and to revisit them from time to time as a group to celebrate what God has done in and through your group, but also to be accountable and sustained in your ministry in the marketplace.

Jesus did not come only to save *souls* ( as important and as precious as that is ),
but also to seek, find and recover *everything* that was lost.

– Ed Silvoso

'For the Son of Man came to seek and save that which was lost.'

– Luke 19:10 (NKJV)

… [let] your Kingdom come, [let] your will be done, on earth as it is in heaven.

– Matthew 6:10

# 4

## MORE THAN JUST A
## CHRISTIAN WHO WORKS

### The Power of a
### Kingdom Mindset in your Work Life

S ome years ago I was visiting an elderly congregation member on his death-bed. He said something that has remained with me. As we talked about his life, discussing both his joys and struggles over the years, he commented that he was sorrier for the things he had not done than the things he shouldn't have done. You know, that is true for me; there are so many things I could have done and should have done, that I simply never did. Sometimes it is poor planning, sometimes life just becomes too busy, and sometimes I just don't have the courage or the commitment to do what needs to be done. Is there anything in your life that you feel you should be doing, or should have done, that you now regret? The good news is that it is not too late to start making the most of the rest of your life! It just takes some intentional planning and a closer relationship with God. For many people the greatest extent of their daily planning is to set their alarm clock so that they wake up on time to go to work.

When we come to realise that every moment of our lives is a precious gift from God, packed with opportunities to be blessed and be a blessing, we begin to treat our time at work differently.

> *When we come to realise that every moment of our lives is a precious gift from God, packed with opportunities to be blessed and be a blessing, we begin to treat our time at work differently.*

When you wake up in the morning and get ready to head off to work God already has a plan for your day and God's plan is a perfect, loving, plan. During the day you will meet people God wants to reach out to, you will participate in events that God wants to have an impact on and influence, and you will have a chance to make a difference for God in an environment where few Christians are doing anything significant for God's kingdom.

Graham and I have come to discover that our time at work is as important to God as our prayer and worship time! Psalm 90:12 says, 'Teach *us* to number our days that we may gain a heart of wisdom' (NKJV). When you come to discover just how precious every minute of your working day is and how important every relationship in your work life is, you begin to plan and act wisely for each day, week, month and year so that God is glorified by your work, and you experience the joy and blessing of living within his will.

## Being a Christian Who Works is Not Enough!

In the previous chapter we discussed how you can take Jesus to work with you. It is important to involve Jesus in every aspect of your life because He cares about every aspect of your life and wants to bless you and help you in every aspect of your life! However, taking your Savior to work with you is not enough. God wants you to be more than just a Christian who has a job! He desires to use you as a minister in your workplace.

> *God wants you to be more than just a Christian who has a job! He desires to use you as a minister in your workplace.*

The English word 'minister' comes from the French *ministre* which means to 'act under the authority of another person.' The term was first used in the English language in the 1300's when servants of the King, called 'ministers', would be sent by the King to deliver messages or represent the King in different circumstances. The Christian church later adopted this term to refer to Christian servants who acted under the authority of Christ their King in their daily lives. It was only much later that the word came to be used for ordained or full-time clergy.

Every Christian should be a minister, a servant, who acts under the authority of Christ the King in his or her daily life. Graham is a marketplace minister because he is gifted for ministry in the marketplace. His abilities, his skills and his life's training has prepared him to act as a minister in the workplace so that God's will can be achieved in him and through him.

It is worth reminding ourselves once more that Colossians 3:23 says, '*Whatever you do*, work at it with all your heart, as working for the Lord, not for men …' God wants every Christian to be a minister in his or her workplace, acting under his authority and guidance, to do more than just the tasks and functions of his or her job, so that God's will can be done on earth as it is in heaven (see Matthew 6:10).

## Why Did Jesus Come?

Let me ask you an important question: Why did Jesus come to earth?

One of the great misconceptions among Christians is that Jesus came only to save people from their sins. Of course Jesus did come to save people, but that is not the primary reason why Jesus came. Luke 19:10 gives us our first clear insight into the reason why Jesus came to earth: 'For the Son of Man came to seek and save *that* which was lost' (NKJV). Have you ever noticed that one little word? Jesus did not only come to save those who are lost, He came to save *that* which was lost – in other words Jesus came to save more than just people. Some translations are even more straightforward in showing that God has a saving concern for everything that exists; they simply read, 'For the Son of Man came to save *what* was lost' (Luke 19:10, NIV).

When we think that Jesus *only* came to save people from their sins, we make the mistake of placing humans at the center of reality. That is sinful in itself. God, and God's will, is always the most important consideration at the center of all reality.

So, let me ask the question again, why did Jesus come to earth? Jesus tells us clearly in Luke 4:43, 'I must preach the good news of the *kingdom of God* to the other towns also, because that is why I was sent'. Jesus' answer to the question is that He was sent to proclaim the kingdom of God. Salvation is critical to God's kingdom because it restores us to the correct relationship with our King. What few Christians realise is that salvation is just the first step of the most exciting journey of your life. The real blessing comes in the steps that follow.

> *What few Christians realise is that salvation is just the first step of the most exciting journey of your life. The real blessing comes in the steps that follow.*

When my children were born I did not leave the hospital after the birth and say, 'Right, now the joy is over, it is time to get on with life.' No, the real joy followed in the years after their birth as they grew, learned to walk, talk and to become the wonderful people God had created them to be.

The same applies to you; the most exciting aspects of your walk with God begin the day you take up the challenge to grow from birth towards Christian maturity.

We have already said that Jesus came to establish God's kingdom. The Bible describes God's kingdom in a wonderful way. Of the many descriptions of God's kingdom I will just share two. The first comes from the Old Testament.

> *The wolf will live with the lamb, the leopard will lie down with the goat, the calf and the lion and the yearling together; and a little child will lead them. The cow will feed with the bear, their young will lie down together, and the lion will eat straw like the ox. The infant will play near the hole of the cobra, and the young child put his hand into the viper's nest. They will neither harm nor destroy on all my holy mountain, for the earth will be full of the knowledge of the LORD as the waters cover the sea.*
>
> – ISAIAH 11:6–9

In the Old Testament God's kingdom is described as an eternal and everlasting 'peace' that will cover the whole earth. This peace, called *Shalom* in Hebrew, is not just an absence of strife and war, rather it is the real presence of God's peace that brings true blessing, security, freedom and life. God wants to establish his eternal *Shalom* on earth, and he wants to use you to do it.

We also read about God's kingdom in the New Testament. One of the best descriptions can be found here:

> *And I heard a loud voice from the throne saying, 'Now the dwelling of God is with men, and he will live with them. They will be his people, and God himself will be with them and be their God. He will wipe every tear from their eyes. There will be no more death or mourning or crying or pain, for the old order of things has passed away.' He who was seated on the throne said, 'I am making everything new!'*
>
> – REVELATION 21:3–5A

Frequently the power of this description is lost because we overspiritualise it, either by thinking that it only refers to some symbolic spiritual reality, or by placing it so far in the future that it becomes nothing more than a long-expected hope. The reality is that God longs to see his kingdom established in the world today, which is why Jesus taught his disciples to pray, '… [let] your kingdom come, [let] your will be done, on earth as it is in heaven' (Matt 6:10). Can you imagine a world in which children are safe; a world in which there is no more war, or famine, or crime; a world in which violence and fear have ended; a world in which 'the old order of things has passed away'? (Rev 21:4)

It is not only possible to see God's kingdom established in our world, but Christians have the privilege of working with God to see it become a reality in their context.

In Revelation 21:24–26 (KJV) we read that 'glory and honour of the nations' will be paraded before the Lord. Think about it, the glory and honour of the nations will certainly include those elements of our national life that honour God (education, healthcare, just laws, societies in which people have homes, jobs, food and so forth).

What you do with your work life in order to establish God's kingdom in a practical way, and what you can encourage every other Christian to do with his or her efforts, skills and commitment, can be brought before the Lord as a sacrifice of worship and honour in the great parade of the nations!

## Some Practical Pointers for Establishing God's Kingdom in Your Workplace

When we look at our work life from a kingdom perspective we can see just how critical it is that we ask for God's guidance, wisdom, strength and power to achieve what God wants done where we work. We must seek God's wisdom, revelation and help to establish God's kingdom where we work. Moreover, it is your joy and responsibility, to get other Christians to join you in this ministry.

You can do many wonderfully creative things in order to establish God's kingdom in your workplace. Here are a few points that you can consider as you get started.

The first and most important thing to understand is that for God's kingdom to be established in your work life, God must first be recognised as king of your life.

A king wants his will to be done in his kingdom – it is the same with God our king. Establishing God as your king may be easier than you think in your work life! In order to make God king of your life you need to make the journey from ONLY seeing Jesus as Savior to ALSO seeing Jesus as Lord.

---

*In order to make God king of your life you need to make the journey from ONLY seeing Jesus as Savior to ALSO seeing Jesus as Lord.*

---

The journey begins with confessing your sins to God and accepting the incredible and immeasurable gift of salvation that comes from having your sins forgiven by Jesus (see Rom 6:23). 'Yet to all who received him, to those who believed in his name, he gave the right to become children of God' (John 1:12). The next step is equally exciting; this is where you start the journey of discipleship!

It is interesting to note that when Jesus sends out his disciples in the great commission He does not just command them to go and make *believers* of all nations, rather He says, 'Go and make *disciples* of all nations …' (Matt 28:19). Most Christians find it easy to relate to Jesus as their Savior, but very few find it easy to relate to Jesus as their Lord. There are not that many Christians who choose to make Jesus their Lord, becoming true disciples of the Lord who seek to live under his *discipline*. What is certain is that the Lord has a perfect will for your life; in fact, Paul describes God's will for your life as '… good, pleasing and perfect' (Rom 12:2). James 1:25 tells of the great reward and blessing that comes from submitting to the will of Jesus our Lord: 'But the man who looks intently into the perfect law that gives freedom, and continues to do this, not forgetting what he has heard, but doing it – he will be blessed in what he does.'

Graham had to make this journey from his heart to his knees in order to make Jesus the Lord of his whole life, including his work life in the Power Group of companies. I can assure you that it took courage and intention to take this step of submitting to Jesus as Lord, so that God's kingdom could be established. Graham had to learn to listen for the voice of God so that God could guide him in his daily decisions. He had to make the time to pray about difficult situations, challenging decisions and difficult people. There were all sorts of challenges he had to overcome in order to submit truly to Jesus as Lord in his work life. He practically had to find the time in his day to pray and read the scriptures specifically to find God's input and guidance for his work. Remember, a marketplace minister works under the authority of God the king! Secondly, he had to find the courage to act upon the decisions that God was telling him to take. It takes courage to follow God's leading; when you first begin you are bound to make some mistakes, but as you grow in the confidence of God's guidance and power this will become easier.

The next step in establishing God's kingdom in your workplace is the crucial step of community. Throughout the Bible and Christian history we can see that God most often works through groups of people. Jesus chose disciples to minister with Him, Paul raised up leaders in every place where he planted a church; the simple truth is that you will get a lot more done for God's kingdom if you can do it with the support and help of other Christians. If you work with other disciples, you have a much better chance of seeing the will and ways of Jesus established in your workplace. Graham had to reach out to other Christians in our company and our industry and ask them to join him in working towards the establishment of God's kingdom. We are so blessed that we now have a community of intercessors, marketplace ministers and Christian friends who pray with us, support us and work with us to see that God's will is done in our company and our industry.

I would encourage you to pray and ask God to show you the Christians that work with you. Once you know who they are, ask God to give you the opportunity and the words to use in approaching them to share your passion to see God's kingdom established in the workplace. It helps to give some prayer and thought to what exactly God may want his disciples to achieve in your context – for example, what elements of Isaiah 11 and Revelation 21 can you help to establish through your work? Share the vision with them, the vision of God's eternal *Shalom*, then get together and start praying about how Jesus would want to use you to influence change in your workplace in a loving and gentle way; to change the way you relate to your co-workers, your employer, your customers and even the other companies and groups that work in your area. You will be surprised at how things change around you when you have the courage and the commitment to establish God's kingdom in your workplace.

> *You will be surprised at how things change around you when you have the courage and the commitment to establish God's kingdom in your workplace.*

Very often the things that God wants done in order to make his kingdom visible and tangible are practical things – when you read Jesus' mission statement for his life's work you can see that Jesus understood that God had sent Him to do some very practical things, such as to bring recovery of sight to blind people, to care for those who were in financial crisis, to offer hope to those who are imprisoned and to proclaim that God's favour rests upon people (Luke 4:18–19).

It is very likely that God wants you to do some practical things in order to see his kingdom established in your workplace.

Let me give you two examples of how we have seen this done in our ministry.

Because God wants the Power Group to 'bow the knee' to Him as Lord we have done a few things, like opening our meetings with prayer and sharing our vision to be a kingdom company with our staff and clients. We also pray over tenders and project plans that we submit for new work. We ask for God's guidance, wisdom and help to get them right (not only to win the work, but also to deliver the best possible results for the client and the community at large). Another thing that we have done is to ask how we can partner God in order to see God's will done in the area of our work which is highway construction and township development. As a result, we have established a charitable trust where we deposit ten percent of our company's profits. We use the money in that trust to do very practical things that help people to experience the *Shalom* of God's kingdom. For example, we fund feeding schemes, we build schools and support educational projects, we support ministries and organisations that offer medication and care to persons who are HIV positive, we help to build houses for the needy and so forth. I don't need to list all the different things that we do here. The simple principle is that we asked God, 'Lord, what do you want to do with us and through us in order to see your kingdom established where we work?' The outcome is that our company has a wonderful vision which is, 'To transform the lives of people in Africa through infrastructure development'.

There are many of our employees within the company who do wonderfully creative and significant things to see God's kingdom established within their sphere of influence. We have many staff members who gather in groups to pray for their co-workers and for their departments. This year the staff of our finance department arranged to build a home for someone with 'Habitat for Humanity' and they gathered canned food and other goods to bless needy families at Christmas. Of course the simplest and most powerful expression of God's kingdom often comes through simply doing one's work with diligence and excellence and giving God all the glory!

What can you do in order to see God's kingdom established where you work?

## God's Kingdom, God's Power and God's Protection

One final point that I want to mention is the simple principle that God desires to protect and empower you to achieve his will in your work life when you choose to submit yourself to God's will. As we read in James 1:25, God blesses the person who looks intently for the will of the Lord and does it. It is fairly certain that we will all face challenges in our work life. Sometimes we may have to face financial pressure, or we may work with a difficult person, or under a difficult boss. What is certain is that God longs to support you and help you in all these situations if you will just ask Him to guide you, lead you and protect you, not for your own gain, but for the sake of his kingdom.

Points to Ponder

Have you ever made the journey from your heart to your knees? It is important that you move from being only a believer in Jesus your Savior to becoming a disciple of Jesus your Lord!

The first thing that I would like to challenge you to do is to find a few minutes and to go on your knees and ask Jesus not only to save you from your sins and restore your relationship with Him, but to become your Lord and master as well, inviting Him to establish his kingdom in your WHOLE life. This is exactly what Graham did one night, alone in his study at home, in 1999. From that one moment on his life began to change.

Here are a few questions to pray about:

- If Jesus were the head of your business or company what would He do differently in order to make his kingdom visible through the work that you do? Remember, a teacher can bring truth to learners, a nurse can bring true healing to sick people, an office worker can ensure that ethics and moral standards are applied in administration, a manager can ensure that just standards are applied in the company policies and a senior leader can ensure that a department or a whole business moves in the direction that God wants them to go.
- What can you commit to do within your sphere of influence? Take a few minutes to pray and ask God to reveal his will and plan for your work life to you. Ask God to show you how He wants you to do you work differently, what He wants you to achieve, how He wants you to interact with your co-workers or clients.
- Who is there in your workplace that can become a kingdom partner with you? Perhaps there are a few other Christians who have not yet risen to the challenge of adopting a kingdom vision for your workplace? Ask God to show you the time and place where you can share the simple principle of God's desire to establish his kingdom with them. It will be even more effective if you can give them some examples of how a kingdom vision in your workplace can transform your environment and bless people and honour God!

- Remember that Jesus not only wants to save you and the people that you deal with every day, He also longs to bless all of you in his kingdom! Jesus wants to be your Savior as well as your Lord! Establishing God's kingdom in any place and relationship is as simple as bowing your knee, your heart and your will to Jesus the King in your meetings, your daily tasks and your interactions.

Questions for Group Discussion
- Why isn't it enough simply to be a Christian who works? What difference does a 'kingdom mindset' make to your work life?
- In this chapter I suggested that in order to establish God's kingdom in your life you will need to take the journey from seeing Jesus ONLY as your Savior, to also seeing Jesus as your Lord. What does it mean to accept Jesus as your Lord? How does this reality transform and change every aspect of your daily life, your decisions, and your actions?
- Please read Isaiah 11:6–9 and Revelation 21:3–5a, and any other verses from the Bible that speak of God's loving and gracious kingdom. Please describe what the world would look like if God's kingdom were established.
- Please read Luke 4:18–19. What makes Jesus' kingdom ministry so practical in transforming the world? What practical things could you do in your work life to manifest God's kingdom?
- Please take some time to pray Jesus' own words for the context in which each of your group members works; '[Let] your kingdom come … on earth as it is in heaven' (Matt 6:10). Ask God to empower you and help you to establish his kingdom in your work life.

Building the church is what Jesus does; Taking his Kingdom all over the earth is
what we're commanded to do.

– Ed Silvoso

Unless we move our base of operations to the marketplace, what we do will be nothing more than a
spiritual parade, never the amphibious landing needed to decide the outcome of the war.

– Ed Silvoso

'… on this rock I will build my church, and the gates of Hades [hell] will not overcome it.'

– Matthew 16:18

# 5

## TO HELL WITH THE CHURCH!

### Being the Church Where it Counts

The title of this chapter may have raised some eyebrows! I am fairly certain that a few people will turn straight to this chapter when they first read the contents page! I hope that is true, because the importance of the church in God's plan for the world and in your ministry in the marketplace, cannot be underestimated.

So, let me start by saying that the church is not incidental to God's plan for the transformation and salvation of the world! In its truest form the church is created by God to be 'salt and light', that is to bring light where there is darkness and to stop decay where the world is falling apart! God's dream for the church is for it to be a powerful instrument of change, directed by Him and used by Him, a force against which the forces of darkness cannot stand. Throughout the history of Christianity the church has been just such an instrument of powerful change. Traditionally when we speak of the church we are talking about all the churches in a collective manner. In popular English the church refers to a building, or meeting place, for Christians. For example, we'll often hear people saying 'I went to church on Sunday', or 'James and Grace were married in the local Anglican Church.' In the New Testament however, the church refers not to a building or meeting place, but to Christians who make up the community of the church. It is for this reason that the church has often been viewed in two ways, as the church gathered (like when we gather for a worship service on a Sunday), and the church scattered (like when the Christians who are the church go into the world on Monday).

In this sense, God has great hopes for the church gathered and the church scattered. He has created it to be his voice, his hands and his heart to love and transform the world.

Sadly, the reality is that most of our contemporary congregations are a far cry from that powerful image! As part of one of the projects that we are involved in, the Global Day of Prayer, we travelled throughout the cities and towns of South Africa. For those who don't know, South Africa has one of the highest professing Christian populations in the world (close to eighty percent of South African citizens indicated that they are Christian in the National Census). However, as our Global Day of Prayer teams travelled the towns and cities they discovered some alarming realities.

Firstly, they discovered that there was not a single town or city in South Africa where more than twelve percent of the population could be in church on Sunday – how did they come to this startling realization? They simply found out how many people live in the area and then compared that to the number of seats in all the churches in the city – most cities could only seat about five percent of their resident population. Then when they spoke to the pastors, ministers and church leaders they discovered that almost none of the churches were full on Sundays. In fact, most of them were only about half to two thirds full in a service of worship. So, that was how we came to discover that the church probably only reaches about two to three percent of the population for one or two hours on a Sunday. This is simply not good enough for what God wants to do in order to transform the world!

---

*... the church probably only reaches about two to three percent of
the population for one
or two hours on a Sunday.*

---

## How Churches Plan to Fail

As pastor of a wonderful local church, I preached, admonished, encouraged and prayed my members into the life of the church for many years. Like most ministers I worked very hard and did my best to fill my Sunday services with eager worshippers, and when I had them in the pews I would craft the best sermons I could in order to get them involved in one of our church's many ministries. Some of the ministries supported the life of the local church (women's groups, men's groups, children's and youth ministries, worship teams, counselling teams, visitors, discipleship programmes  and others). Other ministries were expressly designed to 'reach out' of the church building into our community (evangelism programmes, ministry in schools, ministry in hospitals, caring for the poor and needy and so forth).

One day after a particularly passionate sermon, a friend who is a member of our congregation, posed a very challenging question to me. He asked, 'So, Dion, what would you do if by some miraculous intervention of God they all showed up?' What did he mean? 'Well,' he said, 'what if everyone within a five kilometre radius of our church came to know Christ and arrived on Sunday to start their discipleship training in order to become effective and obedient followers of Christ and servants of the Gospel?' Of course I had to admit that I would not have a clue how to deal with all the thousands of people who would come! We would not have enough space to fit them all into our church buildings, let alone have enough programmes and people to begin to disciple all these eager new converts! Then he said, 'OK, so let's make it easier; what if every one of the 700 people in church this morning responded to your passionate plea to get involved in the ministries of the church? What would you do with them if they all turned up on Monday?' I could just imagine the chaos! I arrive at the church office early on a Monday morning and see cars backed up for miles! There are 700 people waiting to be directed towards some form of ministry, service or mission – and the truth was, we simply didn't have enough ministries to involve all the members of our congregation! You can only run so many men's programmes, women's programmes and youth programmes!

That day I had to admit that I was not leading my church for success, I had been planning for failure … I had never considered that the church that God longed for was a powerful church in which every member of the community could be reached in love and discipled with intention and care. It had never crossed my mind that perhaps the ministries that God wanted my members to be involved in were not just ministries from the church, or even connected to the church, but perhaps He wanted me to prepare them to serve elsewhere.

When you think about your church, could you cope if they all turned up? It is quite challenging to think that very few of our local congregations plan for success.

## Ministry in the Marketplace, Worship, Discipleship and Service as it Should be Done

I am pretty sure that most of our churches have inadvertently planned to fail – we simply have never considered the implications of a powerful move by God! Of course there is an answer to our wonderful dilemma! The answer is that we should find a new way of being church and a new way of doing church. So please, do not misunderstand me, the church is absolutely central to God's plan for the salvation and transformation of the world! God rejoices to see families worshipping together. However, we need to be courageous and honest enough to realise that we need a model of church that can truly reach the world in Christ's love if we are ever going to become all that God longs for us to be!

It is worth noting that when Jesus recruited his first twelve disciples He did not recruit a single priest or leader in the synagogue among them! As Ed Silvoso puts it, 'Jesus designed the church to be a counterculture rather than a subculture.'

> *Jesus designed the church to be a counterculture rather than a subculture.*
>
> — ED SILVOSO

Jesus did not ONLY want to reach 'temple goers' with his message, grace and love. No, He had in mind to work through people in the marketplace, their homes, and places of learning to bring his loving and gracious message to bear on the WHOLE of society! Many of our contemporary churches have become an escape from the world, places where we get away from the world to relate to other Christians and to God.

Did you know that after *Jesus loves me this I know ..., I have decided to follow Jesus ...* is the next best known Christian song in the English speaking world? There is a line in the song that sums up the popular view of contemporary Christianity. It goes, 'The cross before me, the world behind me ...' I think many of us live our Christian lives in that way, turning our back on the world that God desperately wants to love through us.

The Bible gives us a different picture of the direction that a Christian should face – we are called to go into the world and 'make disciples of all nations' (Matt 28:19).

When Paul started planting churches (which we read about in the Book of Acts), the Spirit of God kept leading him into the marketplace (see Acts 18:6). Each time that Paul arrived in a city he would head straight for the local synagogue (see Acts 13:5) and there he would attempt to preach the Gospel. However, in almost every instance he would quickly be kicked out of the synagogue. So, what he would do is reach out to the group of people he knew equally well, business people. Paul was not only a very devout Jew, he was also an exceptional businessman. Paul made tents for a living and so he would set up shop in the city and start sharing the good news of Jesus with the people he met in the marketplace (see Acts 20:33–35). Out of these interactions people were saved, churches were planted and whole communities were transformed.

When I was still a young minister one of my bishops once told me that the local church is meant to be a sending church, not a sitting church. He often remarked, 'The church is meant to build bridges to the world, not walls to keep the world out.' The real purpose of the church is to bring people together in worship and discipleship so that they can be uplifted, transformed and equipped to go into the world and minister.

> *… the local church is meant to be a sending church, not a sitting church … It is meant to build bridges to the world, not walls to keep the world out.*

If you read the account of the establishment and growth of the church in Ephesus you'll see that Paul followed a marketplace strategy in his ministry (see Acts 18–20, and you can also read about this church in the letter to the Ephesians). He built relationships with people in the marketplace and as they came to experience the transforming power of Jesus in their lives, homes and businesses, it created such a stir that everyone in Ephesus and the surrounding areas heard the Gospel (see Acts 19:10)! How many local congregations could say that everyone in their midst has heard the Gospel because of their good work?

There are a couple of valuable lessons to be learnt from Paul's marketplace strategy in Ephesus.

Firstly, as a tentmaker Paul was interacting with people where they needed the Gospel and grace of Christ most: he was ministering to them in the pressure of their work life. Paul could subtly influence, support, care for, help and share the Gospel with the people among whom he worked every day. He did not need to create artificial relationships and hypothetical situations in order to share the power of the Gospel with them, he could simply share Christ's love and grace on the spot! Imagine that if one of his customers came to him and shared news of a sick child, Paul could immediately minister in that situation. Clearly, as people experienced the miracles and blessing of Christ's power, their lives began to change (the establishment of the church in Ephesus is a testimony to this fact).

Secondly, Paul made a tangible and practical impact on the community in which he worked and ministered. As he produced goods he added value to the economy and this, in turn, had an impact on the lives of the people in the community in which he was ministering. We read in Acts 20:34-35 that Paul not only met his own financial needs through his work, but he earned enough money to provide for the needs of others. Tangible and practical expressions of love and provision are one of the marketplace minister's most powerful tools.

So here we see two central principles for establishing the church in the marketplace – we bring the love and message of Jesus to people where they are (rather than expecting them to come to where we are). Secondly, through our work we are able to provide for ourselves and others, thereby giving a very practical expression of God's love. This is the way the church should operate, we should be reaching people for Jesus in their everyday environment. In this way their relationship with Jesus develops naturally in the surroundings in which they live and work every day.

When we establish the church in the marketplace we can disciple people who are saved to deal with the real challenges and issues they face every day. A huge struggle that I faced as a pastor was to try and meet all the diverse and different needs of my congregation within the framework of my church. My congregation consisted of, among others, CEOs and tradesmen, people who worked at home and people who drove into the city to work in corporations. These people faced such diverse daily challenges. I was constantly trying to figure out how to support them in their discipleship in a way that would be helpful as well as meaningful. There was no way that I could cater for all their needs. Sadly, churches often lose members because they simply cannot address the specific individual concerns with intention and depth.

However, if there were groups of Christians who understood that their responsibility was to reach people for Christ where they work daily, and then nurture them to maturity as disciples of Christ, could you imagine how powerful and effective the church would be?

When you take up the challenge to establish the church in the marketplace you are making a decision to BE the church where it matters most!

---

*When you take up the challenge to establish the church in the marketplace you are making a decision to BE the church where it matters most!*

---

# Power in Prayer

Fairly soon after Graham came to know Christ he realised the need for the establishment of the church in the marketplace. Now, let me set the hearts and minds of the pastors at ease before I go any further! What Graham intended to do was not to set up a church in opposition to our local church (or any other local church for that matter). Such thinking is not sensible! Any community of sincerely committed Christian believers that introduces people to salvation in Christ and offers them opportunities for worship, growth and ministry, cannot be counterproductive to God's plan for the church. Moreover, if we are honest, there are very few churches that have a significant and strategic presence in the marketplace. Some of us may offer particular care and support to working people in our churches, but I am certain that many churches do not!

This was certainly the case in the Power Group. There were almost 2000 employees in the Power Group, but there was no single church that had made any effort to support the Christians in that geographic region or in the company intentionally during their working hours. Thankfully, there were some ministries (such as BAG – the Business Action Group) that approached Christians in the company to pray for them and with them, and to offer them teaching and training on basic Christian principles (like reading the scriptures, praying, giving, serving, evangelising and so forth).

Graham wanted, and needed, to be among other Christians. He wanted to have a community of people who could journey with him, and with whom he could journey, during his workweek. So, as a Christian in the marketplace, Graham started extending the work of the church into his sphere of influence. The first thing that he did was to start building relationships and networks with other Christians in the company and the industry. From there he got involved in starting up prayer groups, Bible studies, and he even arranged outreach events. Once a month he would invite a speaker to the Power Group, someone prominent like a Christian sports personality or musician. Then he would invite all the employees of the company, clients and anyone in the area who was interested, to come along over lunchtime. These are wonderful events! At one such event last year more than 200 people came to listen to a Christian business owner, Chuck Ripka. After the talk the line of people waiting for prayer extended right out of our training room into the courtyard. I am certain that over the years hundreds of people have come to salvation at one of these special meetings. Early on in his walk with the Lord, Graham invited me to run the

Alpha Course for his employees and in recent years many other programs have been run, such as the Luke 10 Transformation Course in evangelism, and the Willow Creek Leadership Courses. We also place specific emphasis on training our employees in ethics and of course we have invited groups such as rēp, Consciousness Leadership and 'Doing business God's way' to run courses with our senior management. We have even had sections of our company (like our finance division and development company) that have done practical outreach ministries, like building houses for Habitat for Humanity and collecting food for needy families.

The basic principle is this: Every Christian has the responsibility to establish the ministry of the church within their sphere of influence. This work should support the work of the whole church to the glory of God.

So, if you can start a prayer ministry, or engage in some form of outreach, or just form a group that offers support and study, you are one step closer to making the church the powerful force of transformation that God intends it to be!

## To Hell With the Church!

By now I hope you're asking, 'Where can I begin to establish the church in the marketplace in order to honour God most effectively?' Ed Silvoso sums it up most succinctly when he says that the target of the church should be the world and not the pew.

> *The target of the church should be
> the world and not the pew.*
>
> – ED SILVOSO

One of the most important verses from scripture for the marketplace minister to memorise is this one: '… on this rock I will *build my church*, and the *gates of Hades [hell]* will not overcome it' (Matt 16:18). There are two important lessons that we learn from this passage.

Firstly, we learn that Jesus is the one who builds the church.

I almost burnt myself out as a young pastor trying to build Jesus' church. I spent sixteen hours a day, seven days a week, trying to increase the membership of the church in which I ministered. Sometimes it felt like pushing jelly up a hill! Just as I thought I was getting to the top of the mountain it would slip past me and I would have to start over. I know many church leaders, pastors and members of churches who are trying to build their church, instead of letting Jesus build his church. Graham is a good example of someone who understood the principle that it is Christ who builds his church. What Graham was required to do was to be obedient to what God had called him to, to do that with passion, commitment, creativity and sacrifice, and Jesus would take care of the rest. When Graham focused his attention on being a faithful disciple of Jesus in the marketplace, the other pieces of establishing the church (and even growing the churches like mine, in which his employees worshipped) seemed to fall into place without much effort. As Christians begin to experience and see the power of God at work in their daily lives their commitment to worship, ministry, and outreach grows! Our church experienced a great deal of growth as the ministries related to the Power Group began to be established. Our youth became involved in the 'Walk of Hope' which was related to the Global Day of Prayer. Many of our members are involved in the Global Day of Prayer and Unashamedly Ethical movements. They have joined Christian forums and are themselves taking up their responsibility as ministers in the marketplace. The outcome is that our city, Somerset West, and our church are experiencing the blessing of Jesus building his church much more broadly and effectively than we could have done if we had tried to contain the passions, gifts, and abilities of our members to our congregation.

This leads us to the second lesson that we learn in Matthew 16:18, namely that the church must go to hell! Where is the best place to 'shine your light' and be 'the salt of the earth' (Matt 5:13–15)? You need to shine your light where it is dark of course! For many years I made the mistake of thinking that a church's success is measured by its seating capacity (how many people are in worship on a Sunday). The truth is that a church's salt, its real worth, is measured by its *sending* capacity. God does not care how big the 'salt shaker' is, rather what God is concerned about is how much salt is shaken from the salt shaker, and how much light the church shines in the darkest places of society.

Let me ask you another question, if your church were to close its doors this week, who would notice that you are not in ministry any longer? Of course the members who worship in your congregation would care, but would the homeless in your area notice? Would the hungry and the abused of your society realise that you are not operating anymore? Would your closure have an impact on the sick and the elderly people in your community? How about the schools and businesses in your community; would they notice that you are no longer ministering in the community?

When Jesus said that He would build his church and the gates of hell would not overpower it, there was a clear assumption that He builds his church at the gates of hell! One of the most loving things we can do with the church is to send it to hell. We need to find the places of suffering, brokenness and need, and be the church in those places so that Jesus can build his church there. In my experience those places are not very far from where you work!

## Bread of Heaven

One example of a person who took the church to hell is Andy Loughton, a marketplace minister from our church. Andy loves the Lord, but of equal importance, Andy loves the people that the Lord loves. One of Andy's businesses is a bakery in the center of our town. The area close to the bakery is a popular place for homeless people to congregate.

Remember, as we discussed in the previous chapter, a minister is a servant who operates under the authority of the King. What do you think Jesus would have done if He had been the owner of *Bread of Heaven* bakeries? Of course, He would have used this business to minister to the needy.

Thankfully, Andy thinks as Jesus does, and so in his mind *Bread of Heaven* was a prime opportunity to establish the church in the marketplace! Wherever you have a need and you have a Christian in the same location you can be sure that Jesus wants to do something special. So Andy began to establish the church in a simple way. As a baker he could provide some bread to feed the hungry, but he could also provide the bread of life (see John 6:35). In a place where the churches of our community were seldom active you will now find the church meeting daily. The hungry are fed and the Gospel is preached. *Bread of Heaven* has become a little like the story of Ephesus – so many lives have been changed because of Andy's obedience that many in our community are beginning to hear the good news (as in Acts 19:10).

Points to Ponder
• Where is your church most active? Most of us would probably fit into that three to five percent who experience the church as a place that we go to for an hour or two on a Sunday. God longs to see the church established in the center of the marketplace, just as Graham did in the Power Group and Andy did in *Bread of Heaven*. And the good news is that God is looking to you to do it. Can you imagine what a joy it will be for Graham and Andy to stand before God one day and be able to give an account of what they did with their work life and their business? Paul gives us a wonderful example of how an ordinary working person

can establish the church in the center of the marketplace and in doing so make an incredible impact for the Gospel.

- What steps do you need to take in order to establish the church where you work? It is important to remember that the church is a community of believers who are centred around loving and serving Jesus, but also doing the things that Jesus did. If you want to see such a community formed where you work you will need to find some fellow Christians with whom you can begin praying and sharing. You should also not underestimate the possibility that your pastor, priest, or minister may not have fully understood the need to create a community of Christians outside of your local church. Very few pastors are trained to understand the importance of the marketplace in the church's ministry. You may need to spend some time sharing your vision with him or her, and perhaps even invite your pastor to come and visit you at work and pray with you and your colleagues – Graham did this with me and it made such an impact on my life that I now serve fulltime as a minister within the Power Group. I meet with Andy and a group of local marketplace ministers from time to time to help them strategise how they can keep their pastors and 'sending' congregations on board, while still doing what God has called them to do in the marketplace.

- It is important to remember that Jesus will build his church (see Matthew 16:18). This will mean that you must seek Christ's guidance, help and direction in establishing the church community where you work. Moreover, it may also mean that what the Lord requires from you is quite different from what you are used to. In the Power Group we have people of all sorts of denominations, theological perspectives and church traditions who gather for worship, fellowship, teaching, outreach and prayer. We do our best to avoid theologically controversial issues. We focus rather on growing together in order to honour God where we work. We need all the support and prayer that we can get for this important task. This means that we don't waste time arguing about points of doctrine that are not critical to the task of being the church in the marketplace. I would encourage you to do the same, to be open and hospitable to brothers and sisters from different church denominations. Pray that God will bind you together and give you a common vision for your 'mission field' in the marketplace, then work at it with all your heart!

- Finally, Jesus said that He would build his church at the gates of hell (Matt 16:18). This being the case, where would Jesus want you to begin the work of establishing the church in your context? Where are some of the places of greatest need and struggle in your work life and workplace? Sometimes all it takes is just inviting some Christians to join you in prayer in a place where there is strife and conflict. At other times it may take a practical response, such as what Andy has done in feeding the homeless physically and spiritually. For others it means gathering some funds or foodstuff to care for a colleague who is in need.

Remember, God's intention for the church is that it would be a mighty instrument of salvation, healing and transformation. In order to make that happen we will need to take the Gospel out of our local congregations and into the marketplace. Your workplace may just be the next Ephesus where the testimony of God's grace is so powerful that everyone comes to hear the good news of Jesus (see Acts 19:10).

Questions for Group Discussion
- Please read Matthew 16:18 and Matthew 5:13–15.
- Please discuss some of the places of greatest need in your situation (the darkest places that need light, and the places with the most decay that need preservation). What makes these places so dark and desperate?
- Jesus says that we are to be the light in darkness and the salt in the midst of decay. Can you give some practical examples of instances where you have seen other Christians being salt and light in the world? What difference did their actions, choices and attitudes make to those around them?
- Please consider the ministries of the local churches that the members of your group belong to. Take some time to discuss and celebrate those ministries that are establishing the church at the 'gates of Hades [hell]'. Pray for the people involved in those ministries.
- Please list some places where 'salt and light' are desperately needed where your church is not active. What can you do in order to bring salt and light to those situations, people or places? Try to be as specific and practical as you possibly can in your suggestions.
- Please take some time to pray for the ministry of your church or respective churches. Then pray for one another, asking God to strengthen your witness and give each of you a servant heart and all the resources you will need to be salt and light.

People often talk about the sacred-secular divide, but my faith tells me that God is found in earth and rocks and buildings and institutions, and yes, in the business world.

– David Miller

For the first sixteen years of his ministry, Paul did what most pulpit ministers do today: He preached to God-fearing people in religious settings with notable results. But he did not see a city or a region transformed until he partnered with the marketplace.

– Ed Silvoso

'The Spirit of the Lord is on me, because he has anointed me to preach good news to the poor. He has sent me to proclaim freedom for the prisoners and recovery of sight for the blind, to release the oppressed, to proclaim the year of the Lord's favour.'

– Luke 4:18–19

'Now I want you to know, brothers, that what has happened to me has really served to advance the gospel. As a result, it has become clear throughout the whole palace guard and to everyone else that I am in chains for Christ. Because of my chains, most of the brothers in the Lord have been encouraged to speak the word of God more courageously and fearlessly.'

– Philippians 1:12–14

# 6

## JESUS AND PAUL, A CARPENTER

## AND A TENTMAKER

### God's Prototype for Ministry in the Marketplace

When you think about Jesus, what kind of minister do you think He was? This may sound like a strange question, but it is very important to answer it honestly! I have come to see that most Christians tend to think of Jesus more as a 'monk' than as a 'manager'!

Some of the people that I spoke to thought that Jesus did similar things during his ministry to what their pastor does today (He preached, He cared for the sick, He nurtured people, He built a community). Of course that is partially true – a great deal of what pastors do in their congregations today is modelled on the ministry of Jesus. However, it is a mistake to limit your understanding of Jesus' ministry to such a narrow understanding. The problem with seeing Jesus in this way is that it becomes difficult to imagine that Jesus did the kinds of 'ordinary' things that you and I have to do each day! Somehow this 'religious' view of Jesus and his ministry creates a measure of separation between our everyday lives – and particularly our everyday work lives – and the life and work of Jesus.

In fact, I am sure that, like me, you may have heard some sermons preached in which the impression is created that Jesus is antagonistic towards the marketplace! People who adopt this perspective have often misused the story of the rich young ruler (see Luke 18:18–25), and the account of Jesus driving the merchants out of the temple (see Matthew 21:12–17). In both instances, however, Jesus is not making statements about work and wealth, but rather about greed, priorities and justice.

I could ask you the same question about the apostle Paul – what is your view of Paul's ministry? Most of the people I spoke to seemed convinced that Paul was a 'pulpit' minister i.e., a pastor of different congregations. Some people had heard that Paul was a 'tentmaker', but when I asked them what they understood that to mean, the answers were not all that favourable of Paul's work life. In fact, one of the people said that Paul only worked because he had to, and that if he had a choice he would have left his 'work' and would have been a full-time minister. I have read Paul's letters and the book of Acts many times and I can find no evidence to support such a view. The term 'tentmaker' has taken on a loaded meaning in contemporary English. In effect it means someone who has two vocations, in fact in some churches 'tentmaking ministers' are called 'bi-vocational' ministers. What they mean by this is that people who do this kind of ministry do one thing to earn money (that is their work) and do something completely different as their ministry. Paul was certainly not a 'tentmaker' in this sense of the word.

This chapter will give you a different perspective on the life and ministry of two marketplace ministry prototypes – Jesus and Paul.

## Jesus the Businessman

Our picture of Jesus and his ministry is shaped by years of reading, learning, and thinking about the Savior. I have found that I sometimes need to see things from a slightly different perspective in order to discover new opportunities and possibilities for my faith life.

Let me illustrate it to you in this way. Recently a friend attended a course on 'listening' for a counselling programme he is presenting. The facilitator placed a cereal box in the middle of the table around which the participants were sitting. He asked each of them to tell the others what they saw. Naturally there were various descriptions of the box depending on where the participants were sitting. Some saw the front of the box, while others saw the back. Some could see part of the front and one side, while others could see part of the back and the other side.

What you will read next is simply an attempt to look at Jesus' life from a different angle – an angle that might help you to feel closer to Him in your everyday work life.

Biblical scholars tell us that Jesus lived for about thirty-three years (from his birth to his death on the cross). During those thirty-three years the synoptic Gospels record that Jesus only spent three years of his life, from the age of thirty to thirty-three, doing the kind of ministry that makes most people view Him as a wandering monk or Rabbi (Hebrew teacher or priest). Have you ever thought about what Jesus did with the rest of his life? Did Jesus only start loving people, praying for them, caring for their needs, telling them about God when He turned thirty? Of course not! While Jesus may only have started his public 'teaching' ministry at around thirty years of age (see Luke 3:23; 4:14–15), we know that He was already displaying the evidence of his special nature and calling as a young boy. Luke says 'And the child grew and became strong; he was filled with wisdom, and the grace of God was upon him.' (Luke

2:40). How would others have known of his wisdom unless He was saying and doing wise things? How would they have known that God's grace was upon Him unless He was already displaying God's grace in his words and actions? In fact, the clearest evidence that Jesus was already engaging in ministry as a boy is to be found in Luke 2:41–52, the account of Jesus engaging the priests in conversation in the temple. Once again this passage ends with Luke noting, 'And Jesus grew in wisdom and stature, and in favour with God and men.' (Luke 2:52).

So, we can be sure that Jesus was a minister, even as a young child – (see Luke 2:49) Jesus notes that He is going about his Father's business. As we discussed in chapter 4, to be a minister means to 'act under God's authority'. It is assumed that Jesus would have been about twelve years of age when this incident in the temple took place and, as Luke points out, He continued to grow in stature, getting recognition from others. He found great favour with God and other people.

This simply means that Jesus was engaged in a different form of ministry from at least age twelve to thirty, than the kind of ministry He practised from age thirty to thirty-three. What kind of ministry was Jesus engaged in during those eighteen years? Mark's Gospel gives us an insight into the primary way in which Jesus' community viewed Him during that period, 'Isn't this the carpenter? Isn't this Mary's son and the brother of James, Joseph, Judas and Simon? Aren't his sisters here with us?' (Mark 6:3–4).

Jesus' contemporaries recognised Him first as a businessman – a carpenter – and then only later as their teacher and savior.

---

*Jesus' contemporaries recognised him first as a businessman – a carpenter – and then only later as their teacher and savior.*

---

It is important to note that Jesus did not do carpentry as a hobby. In the ancient Near East a boy would take up his trade as a teenager, normally learning the skills and techniques that he would use to support his family in years to come. Since Joseph was a carpenter, Jesus followed the same trade. So by the time Jesus began his public ministry (see Luke 3:23) He had spent almost twenty years applying his trade. Of course it is not surprising that his contemporaries found it difficult to relate to Him as their Savior, since some of them would have bought Jesus' products! Perhaps they had a table, or a door, or some farm implement that Jesus had crafted for them in their house. Furthermore, Jesus clearly knew his trade well, since we can see that He uses the metaphor of a wooden yoke, something that a skilled carpenter would have made many times, to illustrate the blessing of living a life under submission to God (see Matt 11:29–30). As Ed Silvoso rightly points out in *Anointed for Business*, Jesus' parables are full of examples that show his understanding of business and the marketplace: construction (see Matt 7:24–27), wine-making (see Luke 5:37–38), farming (see Mark 4:2–20), tending animals (see Matt 18:13–44), management and labour (see Matt 20:1–16), return on investments (see Matt 25:14–30), crop yield (see Mark 13:27–32) and management criteria (see Luke 12:35–48).

Just as Jesus confronted people with the knowledge of business then, He wishes to confront you with the knowledge of your daily work today! Jesus understands the pressures of working with people, the challenge of creating something that one can market and sell in order to earn a livelihood. Jesus knows how to deal with customers and suppliers, how to manage a workflow and juggle priorities in order to remain in business – He did it for twenty years of his life. And, the remarkable thing about it is that we are told that while He did this he continued to grow in wisdom and favour with both God and people! Jesus understands what it means to be a minister in the marketplace.

Central to Jesus' ministry in the marketplace was the understanding that He needed to obey God's will in order to establish God's kingdom on earth. Notice that Jesus' mission statement is very practical. It deals with poverty, health care, criminal reform, debt, justice and God's loving favour (Luke 4:18–19). In order to be an effective minister in the marketplace Jesus had to have two primary orientations:

- Firstly, Jesus had to acknowledge that God had a will for every aspect of his life. In other words, God wanted to use Jesus as much in the marketplace as He used Him in the temple. God's will runs throughout the whole of Jesus' life! Everything that Jesus did was ministry! In order to know and operate within God's will, Jesus had to set aside time to listen for God's voice, to discover God's guidance and leading and to be strengthened and equipped to face every challenge – even death, in order to bless and please God.

---

*In order to know and operate within God's will, Jesus had to set aside time to listen for God's voice, to discover God's guidance and leading and to be strengthened and equipped to face every challenge.*

---

- Before Jesus did his work – his ministry – He took time to pray and seek God's presence, 'Very early in the morning, while it was still dark, Jesus got up, left the house and went off to a solitary place, where he prayed' (Mark 1:35). How much time do you spend in prayer, asking God to guide and lead you into situations, or relationships, that can benefit your ministry in the workplace? As I mentioned in the practical pointers in Chapter 2, I have a simple little discipline – each Sunday evening I look through my date book and pray over every meeting, every person that I will meet, every challenge and every opportunity that I will face in that week. I bring the people, the tasks, the pressures and the decisions before God for his help, his guidance, and his will. Jesus is my 'line manager', so I have that little 'meeting' with Him to tell Him about my week and ask his advice and direction for the week. Remember Paul's instruction? 'Whatever you do, work at it with all your heart, as working for the Lord, not for men … It is the Lord Christ you are serving' (Col 3:23–24).

- Secondly, Jesus had to capitalise on every opportunity in the marketplace in order to see God's kingdom established. Relationships are central to a Godly influence in the marketplace! There is little doubt that long before Jesus started preaching about God's kingdom He had already added great value to the lives of people He met, finding tangible ways to bless people through his abilities and skill. It is for this reason that people described him as a businessman before they recognised Him as a teacher (see Mark 6:3). Jesus was willing to visit with the wealthy (see Luke 11:37, 14:7, 19:5) and with the poor. Jesus was well-informed on the events of the cities and towns He visited, therefore He understood the economic and political challenges that people faced. However, his primary objective was always to bring God and God's will into every situation. He turned a food shortage into a testimony of God's power (see Matt 14:13–21), and the embarrassment of insufficient catering at a wedding into an opportunity to give glory to God (see John 2:1–10). Jesus used every opportunity to bring people and situations into God's spotlight, so that they could be blessed, transformed and aligned with the principles of God's kingdom. What situations, relationships and opportunities can you use more wisely in order to bring people and structures into a closer relationship with God, and establish God's kingdom in your sphere of influence?

So, when we consider Jesus' ministry from this angle we can see that He truly is a 'prototype' of a minister in the marketplace! Not only does He understand what you are facing each day, but He has modelled how you can transform your ordinary workday into an extraordinary calling!

## Paul – from the Pulpit to the Marketplace

When you make the choice to do 'whatever you do' (Col 3:23) for Jesus, you will soon learn that the dividing line between ministry and work disappears! Graham came to discover this as he realised that he did not need to be a preacher, or a church leader in order to be in ministry. Graham's ministry is running the Power Group of companies and using his gifts, talents, abilities, influence and passion for Jesus to encounter and transform people and institutions in society.

Paul's ministry in the marketplace also took shape as he submitted himself to the leading of the Spirit and learned to minister where God placed him.

Paul started out his ministry as a Jewish Rabbi – in fact this was before his encounter with Jesus on the road to Damascus (see Acts 9:1–19). Paul describes his training and passion in Philippians 3:5, 'circumcised on the eighth day, of the people of Israel, of the tribe of Benjamin, a Hebrew of Hebrews; in regard to the law, a Pharisee'. Because of this background in the Hebrew faith it seemed natural for Paul to continue his ministry, when he came to Christ, by preaching salvation in the synagogues. Each time that Paul entered a city he would head straight for the synagogue to share the good news of Jesus (see Acts 13:5 – Salamis; 13:14–16 – Antioch; 14:1 – Iconium; 17:1–3 – Thessalonica; 17:10 – Berea; 17:16 – Athens; 18:1–4 Corinth; 18:19 – Ephesus).

However, God had an entirely different plan for Paul! Each time that he tried to convince the Jews that Jesus was the promised Messiah they would kick him out of the synagogue. So here was a 'converted' Rabbi who could not find a congregation to preach to! What was he to do? God's strategy for ministry is often much more effective than our plans and ideas of how things should be done.

Here are a couple of problems with Paul's 'pulpit' strategy:

• Paul needed approval to preach. Before Paul could share the good news of Jesus with his audience he would first need to get their acceptance, and possibly even their permission to speak. This is a 'hit-and-miss' strategy, since, as we can see in Acts, Paul seldom found a kind ear, an open mind and a receptive heart in the synagogue.

• Paul's ministry was limited in time and location. If Paul's strategy had worked he would only have been able to preach the Gospel in synagogues during the times of their meetings each week. That is not a very effective way to start a radical new movement that will sweep the whole earth! I don't know about your experience of the local church, but I have seldom found many passionate people in my local congregations who are willing to 'run with the message' after they have heard it! They are much more likely to invite you back to talk it through, ask some questions, get clarity on some of the finer points, and then possibly make a small commitment to help you in their spare time. Does that sound familiar? Thank goodness Paul's strategy did not work.

- Finally, and this is the one I am most thankful for, Paul's strategy was limited to one group of people – the Jews. If Paul had only preached in the synagogues (as was his intention) he would only have brought Jewish believers to faith in Christ. The Gentile population of the world (which includes me) would never have been reached, the Christian church would never have been born, and the majority of the world's population would be lost in sin. Thankfully, God's Spirit gave Paul another strategy!

God's strategy for Paul was to multiply his influence, increase his reach and place him in an energised and explosive environment where the Gospel could spread rapidly and effectively throughout the whole world, to all people, in all situations. Here is a little fact that you may not be aware of – did you know that the Book of Acts records forty supernatural events? Of these forty supernatural events thirty-nine take place in the marketplace (homes, secular buildings, communal spaces, town squares and so forth). Isn't that remarkable? If you want to read more about this, please see Ed Silvoso's book *Anointed for Business* (Regal books, 2002: p 115–118).

The reality is that if we want to transform the world we will need to spend our energy doing the right things in the right places!

---

*The reality is that if we want to transform the world we will need to spend our energy doing the right things in the right places!*

---

People are most often transformed by relationships, not just ideas. When people ask me to introduce myself I often comment that I am a 'recovering academic' – I spent a whole season of my life as a full-time university lecturer. During that time I realised that my ideas were a lot less effective in transforming my students than in building transforming relationships with them. Those students that I got to know and journey with showed a lot more change and transformation than those that just listened to my lectures or read my books! God had to do exactly the same with Paul. If he had simply preached to those people who gathered in great numbers at the synagogue he might have had some very lively theological debates, and spent days considering the finer points of the Prophets and the Law. However, when God sent him into the marketplace he encountered people who were looking for real world solutions to their everyday problems. These were people who wanted to know how they could create meaning in the midst of struggle and how they could find love and happiness within their lifetimes. These were people that longed for a real encounter with someone who loved them and had only their best interests at heart.

So, God sends Paul into the marketplace and the fruit of his ministry is so effective that we read that not only cities are transformed, but whole regions (see Acts 19:10)!

What are some of the principles that we learn from Paul's ministry in the marketplace?

- Relationships are critical to marketplace ministry. One of the clearest examples of this is Paul's relationship with two marketplace ministers that he meets in Corinth, Aquila and Priscilla (see Acts 18:2). These two share the same trade as Paul and so when Paul arrives in Corinth he starts a business with them. Through their strengths as business people Paul's ministry is established. Their credibility helps Paul to build relationships and find favour and open doors in the marketplace, thus he not only earns his living, but also finds an audience with whom to share the good news of Jesus Christ! Relationships are important.
- Paul operates within the scope of his abilities and gifts. God never wastes learning, experience and ability! Since Paul was trained in theology and public speaking, God uses those gifts, but in a different way and in a different place. Paul was primarily a preacher and so he continued to preach. However, his association with marketplace ministers taught him to think out of the box! He did not need the permission, or the location, of the synagogue to preach Christ. He could do it in a town square, or one-on-one with a client, or in a home over dinner, or during a meeting. Paul could share Jesus wherever he was, and his business relationships and credibility in the business community opened those doors to him. We have also experienced this aspect in the Power Group – the fact that Graham is

a very successful businessman gives him a great deal of leverage with other business people. He often gets invited to speak on topics ranging from ethics to entrepreneurship, and from leadership to management. He will use these platforms as an opportunity to proclaim the love and will of Jesus.

• This leads to the third lesson we learn from Paul, namely that sometimes a great failure becomes God's biggest triumph! As a pastor I can only imagine how painful it must have been for Paul to have been brushed off by his colleagues, at best, and driven out by others, at worst! However, Paul's determination was clear – his task was to preach Christ and make Him known! Paul used every single opportunity to preach Christ – when he was chained to the elite Praetorian guards, he thought to himself, 'Great, I'm chained to a guard, this is a captive audience! Now I can preach Christ to him'. Just listen to this, 'Now I want you to know, brothers, that what has happened to me has really served to advance the gospel. As a result, it has become clear throughout the whole palace guard and to everyone else that I am in chains for Christ. Because of my chains, most of the brothers in the Lord have been encouraged to speak the word of God more courageously and fearlessly' (Phil 1:12–14). You may have come through a failure in business. However, God does not want to waste your skill, your abilities and your passion. How can God use you in new and different ways to make the very most of every opportunity to achieve his will in and through your life? God wanted to use Paul's skills, abilities and passion, but He wanted to use them in a different way and in a different place. A slight change in Paul's location and focus made all the difference to his ministry in the marketplace! What might God want for you?

## Points to Ponder

In this chapter we have seen two magnificent prototypes of marketplace ministry – Jesus and Paul. In both instances we gained a completely different perspective on their life and ministry by approaching them from a unique angle. The reality is that we get pressed into the mould of seeing life in the same way that everyone else does. Every now and then it helps to think outside of the box!

• *Invite Jesus into your work life.* The first thing we discussed was that Jesus understands work – He was a working person for most of his life. Have you invited Jesus into your work life? Please take some time in prayer to invite Jesus into your work life now. Invite Him to join you in the place where you work. Invite Jesus to begin to influence your choices, your decisions, and your interactions with people and systems during your work week.

- *Set up a regular meeting with Jesus.* If we are serious about doing everything for Christ, then it is important to allow Him the space to direct our daily lives! Just as Jesus took time to pray and ask God for insight, power and direction, you and I also need to set aside a regular period of time during which we will pray about work and intentionally search the Scriptures for insights, guidance and strength for our work life. Jesus lived his life according to his Father's will. Do you know what God's will is for today? How about for this week, or this year? Be assured that God wants to do some things in you and through you. It is important that you discover God's will for your work life. Without it you will not find peace and purpose. I would suggest that you adopt the discipline of taking thirty minutes on a Sunday to pray about what lies ahead during your work week.
- *Make the most of every opportunity for ministry.* Both Jesus and Paul teach us that we need to make the most of every opportunity to engage in ministry. Are there any opportunities for ministry that you have not yet taken up? Is there a space that God is creating for you in which you can exercise some influence, or facilitate a Godly change *among your co-workers, or in your work place?*
- *Establish deep and significant relationships.* As author John Maxwell says, 'You can impress people from a distance, but you can only impact them up close'.

---

*You can impress people form a distance, but you can only impact them up close.*

— JOHN C. MAXWELL

---

- God has placed you among people that play a critical role in achieving his will in your life and in theirs. Imagine how different Paul's ministry would have been if he had never met Aquila and Priscilla. Jesus sought out people in whose lives He could make a difference and through whose lives He could extend a Godly influence. In God's kingdom things seldom happen outside of a community. To whom can you draw closer so that God can use you more effectively for ministry in the marketplace?

## Questions for Group Discussion

- Please read Acts 18:1–12.
- How different do you think the world would have been if Paul had only preached Jesus in the synagogues?
- It must have taken great courage to move from the synagogue into the market-place (a home) to preach the Gospel. What do you think gave Paul that measure of courage?
- If you were to 'think out of the box' – in what ways could you be more strategic and effective as a minister in the marketplace, as opposed to only ministering in and through your local congregation?
- Please read Mark 1:35–38
- Why do you think Jesus withdrew to pray?
- In what ways do you think this discipline, or withdrawing to pray about your work life, could help you in your ministry in the marketplace?
- Please take some time to consider what relationships and opportunities God is placing before you in your workplace or work life. Please pray for yourself and for other members of your group. Ask God to guide and lead you so that you may be used to transform your city, your region and your nation.

The real test of a man [or woman] is not how well he plays the role he invented for himself,
but how well he plays the role that destiny assigned to him.

– Vaclav Havel

Do you not know that in a race all the runners run, but only
one gets the prize? Run in such a way as to get the prize. Everyone who competes in the games
goes into strict training. They do it to get a crown that will not last; but we do it to get a crown that will
last forever. Therefore I do not run like a man running aimlessly; I do not fight like a man beating the
air. No, I beat my body and make it my slave so that after I have preached to others,
I myself will not be disqualified for the prize.

– 1 Corinthians 9:24–27

Teach us to number our days aright, that we may gain a heart of wisdom.

– Psalm 90:12

# 7

## THE JOURNEY FROM SUCCESS TO SIGNIFICANCE

### Living with the End in Mind

When my wife Megan and I first got married we did not have a clue about budgets and how to manage our meagre income! In fact, for the first few months of our marriage we often 'ran out of money before we ran out of month'. There were numerous months when we simply did not have enough money to see us through to the end of the month because we had not spent our money wisely.

We soon came to realise how important it is to keep the whole month in mind when we received our salaries at the beginning of the month.

Paul gave similar advice to the Christians in Ephesus when he said, 'Be very careful, then, how you live – not as unwise but as wise, making the most of every opportunity, because the days are evil. Therefore do not be foolish, but understand what the Lord's will is' (Eph 5:15–17). The Psalmist said something similar, 'Teach us to number our days aright, that we may gain a heart of wisdom' (Ps 90:12).

Simple stated, we are foolish when we do not consider the value of each day; wasting time, energy, creativity and passion on things that do not really matter. In order to live the best possible life, a life that honours the God who created us with a purpose, and in order to find peace and blessing within ourselves, we have to be intentional about how we live. What we achieve with our lives is most frequently a matter of our choices and the courage to see things through. The following well-known quote sums this sentiment up most clearly for me, 'Failing to plan is planning to fail' (Winston Churchill).

Over the years I have used a simply exercise to help people realise how important it is to take responsibility for directing their lives towards the goal that God has for them. I ask them to sit down and write their own eulogy. This may sound strange, but it is very effective! A eulogy is the tribute that others will pay to your life on the day that you are buried.

Have you every wondered what people will say about you and your life on the day that you die? What will be their lasting memory and impression of you? It is quite challenging to consider this question, but it is important – when we realise that our time on earth is precious, and that every action and interaction has the opportunity to honour God and bless other people, it changes the way we think and live.

> *'The thing is to understand myself, to see what*
> *God really wishes me to do … to find the idea for*
> *which I can live and die.'*
>
> — SØREN KIERKEGAARD

Living with the end in mind is one of the most challenging journeys you will ever undertake, but you will soon discover that it is also one of the most rewarding journeys in life. Are you spending the precious hours of your life wisely? Maybe it is time to make a few changes.

## It's about Obedience!

Have you every wondered why Bill Gates, arguably one of the most successful entrepreneurs of our age, would give up his position at the head of Microsoft in order to join his wife, Melinda, in fighting the spread of malaria in Africa?

I am sure we all know of a friend or relative, who 'packed in' their lucrative job to start over in a lesser-paid position with greater freedom and personal reward?

But let me ask an even more direct question – why do you look through the career and jobs section of the newspaper every so often in the hope of finding some kind of work that will bring you more joy, peace and fulfilment?

For most people the answer is that they long to spend their lives doing something that is truly worthwhile, something that truly matters, something that makes a difference for them and for others.

In the movie *Pearl Harbor*, there is a scene in which Rafe (played by Ben Affleck) says to an English officer: 'I'm not anxious to die sir, just anxious to matter'. We all long to matter; we long to leave a legacy and live a life of true significance. For many of us our working life is a fairly selfish pursuit. It often has to do with applying our gifts, abilities and efforts to achieve what we want and need out of life. We work harder, longer and smarter so that we can see benefit from the rewards of our sacrifice and labour.

True significance, blessing and peace can only come from being the person that God has created you to be, and doing what God wants you to do. All other pursuits may give you some reward, such as wealth, power, or position, but they will never bring lasting satisfaction. When you have worked yourself to a standstill in order to buy a smarter car, you will soon come to realise that there is a better model than you have just bought, waiting in the showroom.

As my friend Brett Johnson reminded me, success and significance are not mutually exclusive categories! In fact, your success can be extremely significant. The key to a life of 'successful significance' is radical obedience to the will of Christ – doing what God wants most with your life. This means that you should aspire for great things and work hard in order to achieve Godly success. However, in this journey it is important you are extremely careful that you do not run the race for 'a crown that will not last'; rather, you should 'run in such a way as to get the prize … a crown that will last forever' (1 Cor 9:24–25).

## What Happens when Your Work does not work for you Anymore?

By the age of forty, Graham had achieved most of his dreams and goals. He had a thriving business, he owned a beautiful home, he had cars, boats, game farms and many of the other rewards of success. However, by his own admission he was not fulfilled. When he speaks to groups of business people he often tells them, 'more companies, bigger deals, more turnover, more game farms, smarter cars, none of these things filled the void I had in my life'. George Bernard Shaw once commented, 'There are two sources of unhappiness in life. One is not getting what you want; the other is getting it'. The simple truth is that there is no title, award or possession that could completely fulfil the purpose for which you were created. The Psalmist says it so clearly: 'Unless the LORD builds the house, its builders labour in vain. Unless the LORD watches over the city, the watchmen stand guard in vain. In vain you rise early and stay up late, toiling for food to eat – for he grants sleep [provision / peace] to those he loves' (Ps 127:1–2).

Like so many other successful people, Graham had come to realise the profound truth that no person could ever find true peace and blessing while they are living for themselves and their own aspirations! A life that is directed towards success, places you and your will ate the center, whereas alife that is directed towards significance, places God and God's will at the center.

*A life that is directed towards success, places you and your will at the center, whereas a life that is directed towards significance, places God and God's will at the center.*

In order to make the journey from doing what Graham wanted to do, towards doing what Jesus wanted him to do, Graham had to make some changes in his personal life and his work life.

One of the mistakes that Christians frequently make when they come to the realization that they need to shift from success to significance is the mistake of thinking that if they give away more money they will find greater blessing and peace. Of course there is nothing wrong with blessing individual persons and groups with your finances; in fact, if God calls you to bless someone you would be wise to do so generously. However, the principle is this – significance comes when you find a way of giving yourself to God!

It takes a lot of courage to commit yourself to living your life for God's purposes and plans rather than your own desires and will. If you are living your life for success, all your choices and decisions are directed at what will be of greatest value to you and your career. However, if your life is directed towards significance, you may have to make some changes in order to direct your life towards God's purposes and plans.

The Power Group is very good at what it does – constructing roads and highways, and building townships and commercial buildings. By doing this the Power Group had grown in prominence in the industry and it was earning good profits. This success started attracting the attention of investors who were eager to buy into Power. Graham had to make a very tough decision at that stage – if he had sold off the controlling share in the company he would have become a very wealthy man instantly. However, the problem would have been that he would be giving over control of the Power Group to the interests of the shareholders. What if he had sold the company and God had then asked Graham to change a certain business practice, or take on a deal or client that would tie up resources but would not return the highest possible profits? If he no longer owned the controlling share in the Power Group he may have a great deal of personal wealth, but would he be able to be obedient to God?

Graham had to consider seriously what mattered most, making a lot of money, or honouring God through the Power Group. Thankfully, Graham had the courage to say that God's will is more important than his own, and so he chose not to sell the Power Group. This decision has been an incredible testimony to many Christians who have faced similar challenges of choosing between success and significance.

Of course this does not mean that a Christian must never sell his or her business, or that a Christian should not leave his or her current position for the sake of a promotion. What is crucial is to seek to be absolutely obedient to God and God's will in every situation. In doing so you honour God with all that you have and all that you do.

*'You may say to yourself, "My power and the strength of my hands have produced this wealth for me." But remember the LORD your God, for it is he who gives you the ability to produce wealth, and so confirms his covenant, which he swore to your forefathers, as it is today'*

– Deuteronomy 8:17–18

## From Construction to Transformation

Today the Power Group has a wonderful purpose, 'Guided and braced by the hand of God, our purpose as a group is to improve the quality of life in Africa through infrastructure development'. So, while we are a company that builds roads and buildings, our God-given purpose is to transform the lives of people in our community by developing necessary infrastructure. This vision allows every member of our staff to understand that he or she plays an integral part in God's calling for the company – from Graham and the other senior executives who offer leadership and management, to the person who digs the trenches and lays the concrete; from the clerk who keeps the records, to the person who cleans the offices, each one is involved in supporting Power in achieving the significance towards which God has called the company.

God clearly had a far greater plan for Graham than just being another wealthy businessman – God wants to use him to leave a legacy. God has a wonderful plan for your life as well. God created you with very special gifts, talents and abilities in order to achieve something special, something significant (see Psalm 139:16).

I have often heard Graham challenging our staff with the question 'God has given you talents and opportunities – what does He expect you to do with them? Graham will have to answer for what he was given, and I will have to give an account for what God has given me, and make no mistake, you will have to answer for the talents you have and the opportunities that God is giving you.

The amazing discovery that I have made over the years, as we saw with Graham's story, is that Godly success often does not require you to do different things; rather, it requires you to do things differently.

---

*Godly success often does not require you to do different things; rather, it requires you to do things differently.*

---

In order for you to honour God more intently, or bless your family with more love, or witness to your colleagues and friends with greater effectiveness, you may just need to become a little more intentional about how you do things. For Graham it meant making some critical choices about his personal values and the reason why he is in business. For you it may require being more patient with a co-worker, or more diligent at a certain task. It may require you to change some of your work habits, or to choose to spend more of your time and money in service of others.

Towards the end of the parable of the talents in Matthew 25 we read these wonderful words, 'Well done, good and faithful servant! You have been faithful with a few things; I will put you in charge of many things. Come and share your master's happiness!' (Matt 25:23).

'Come and share your master's happiness', surely that must be one of the most wonderful affirmations to hear from the Lord when you are called to give account of what you've done with your life!

Points to Ponder
- If you are serious about transforming your life from living only for your own desires and dreams, towards living for the goals and ideals that God has created you for, then it is time to do something about it! Why not get a notepad and a pencil and write the eulogy that you would like to hear at your life's end? This simple exercise could help you to reshape your current choices and values significantly as you journey from success to significance.

  » Firstly, what would you like God to say about your life on that day? I, for example, would love to hear the Lord say something like, 'I am pleased with Dion. He loved me with his whole heart and showed it in every aspect of his life. He used every talent and gift that I gave him to show his love for Me and to the world I love so much. Dion had the courage to follow Me when others did not …' Remember that God has a dream for your life (Psalm 139:16) and He wants you to live your life so that you can share in his joy (Matt 25:23).

» Secondly, what would you like your family to say about you? What would your wife or husband say about your life and your relationships – more importantly, what would you like them to say? Write down what you would like your children to say about you as a parent. These desired outcomes should influence the way in which you spend time with your spouse and children; they should change the way in which you show your love and commitment to them.

» Thirdly, what would your colleagues at work say about you? How would you like them to remember your life? Try to be as specific as possible in what you write here. These points can be very helpful in shaping your ministry among the people that you work with!

» Lastly, what would you like to say about the way you lived your life? I know that I would like to say that I lived my life to the full, that I loved deeply and passionately and that I was prepared to take risks to find blessing and be a blessing to others. I would like to look back on my life and say that it was a life of significance; a life worth living! But in order for this to happen I have had to make some changes to what I do during my work life and during my free time.

---

*Unless a person takes charge of them, both work and free time are likely to be disappointing.*

— MIHALY CSIKSZENTMIHALYI

---

- Having taken the time to consider where you would like to be when your life comes to an end, it is important to take stock of where you are now and then commit to make some changes. What do you need to change in order to finish your life well? It is important to realise that you probably won't be able to change everything in an instant. Rather, you need to set some achievable and realistic goals for what you can change today. It may be something as simple as showing appreciation to a loved one or friend, or asking forgiveness from someone you have upset. Next, consider what you would like to do differently and where you would like to be in a year's time. These goals may take some extra planning and support. Graham, for example, decided that he would like to spend two hours a day in prayer and quiet. This was not something that he could achieve overnight. However, he has slowly worked this time into his diary. It was a significant goal that took some time and effort to achieve, but it was worth it. Finally, consider what you would like to change in the longer term – what would you like to do differently five years from now? Graham wanted to spend more of his time working for ethics and values in the marketplace, so he had to make some commitments to change his personal habits, put some structures in place in his work life and personal life, and also learn as much as he could through prayer and study about these areas. Remember that 'failing to plan is planning to fail', therefore, set yourself some longer-term goals and be as practical as you can about what it will take to achieve them.

- In conclusion, it is worth being reminded that your life is a precious gift that can only be enjoyed and celebrated once. What you choose to do with this day matters to God since it shapes your destiny! I pray that you will have the courage to make wise choices – to choose to journey from success to significance.

Questions for Discussion
- Please read Ephesians 5:15–17 and Matthew 25:13.
- Please list some of the characteristics of a life that is lived for the ideals of 'success'. How do these characteristics differ from a life that is lived for significance?
- What makes a person's life truly significant? Can you give any texts from the Bible to support your understanding of significance?
- Do you think it is possible to be BOTH successful and significant in your work life? Please read Matthew 6:33. Can you list any examples of people who have lived significant lives by God's standards, and have at the same time also been a success?
- In this chapter I said that God has a dream for each person's life. God has a dream for the lives of every person in your group. Why do we find it so difficult to 'live for God's dream' and so much easier to chase our own dreams? What can we do in order to live fully and intently within God's dream and desire for our lives.

Far too frequently Christians feel trapped by the need to earn a living and fulfil their obligations, and we find we struggle to find the courage to live our lives differently from what is 'the norm' in society. God desires the very best for each of us (John 10:10)! Please take some time to pray for one another in the group. Ask God to empower you to live lives of greater significance, lives that achieve God's purpose and lives that will allow you to hear the words, 'Well done, good and faithful servant! You have been faithful with a few things; I will put you in charge of many things. Come and share your master's happiness!' (Matt 25:13)

'Preaching the good news without love is like giving someone a good kiss when you have bad breath. No matter how good your kiss, all the recipient will remember is your bad breath.'

– Ed Silvoso

'People don't care how much you know until they know how much you care.'

– John C. Maxwell

'When you enter a house, first say, "Peace to this house." If a man of peace is there, your peace will rest on him; if not, it will return to you. Stay in that house, eating and drinking whatever they give you, for the worker deserves his wages. Do not move around from house to house. When you enter a town and are welcomed, eat what is set before you. Heal the sick who are there and tell them, "The kingdom of God is near you."'

– Luke 10:5–9

# 8

## THE BIGGEST CHANGES COME THROUGH LOVE!

## Learn How to Show it, How to do it!

A few weeks ago I was speaking to a friend about evangelism and he shared a statistic that shocked me! Apparently less than four percent of Christians will ever share their testimony with another person in a meaningful and intentional way during their lifetime. Think about that for a moment – ninety-six out of every hundred Christians will never tell anyone about the saving and transforming love of Jesus during their lifetime! Let me ask you, 'When last did you share the Gospel of Jesus with another person?'

It is a great mistake to think that the majority of people come to faith in Jesus through crusades and evangelistic outreaches. Of course these events are very effective! But when last did you attend an event like this? How often do they happen in your town or city? Or, even more importantly, when last did you actually invite someone to go with you to a church service of evangelistic outreach?

Just ask ten of your Christian family members or friends who introduced them to Jesus – I am fairly certain that the majority of them will tell you that they came to know of Christ's love through a close friend or family member. It is a simple reality that most people come to experience the truth of the Gospel through loving people and acts of blessing and service long before they are convinced by theological truths such as the divinity of Jesus and the concepts of salvation and forgiveness through faith.

*Faith is most often caught, not taught.*

# Why is it so Difficult to Witness to Jesus' Love?

If it is true that evangelism through close relationships is so effective then why don't more Christians witness to their family, friends and colleagues in this way? I spoke to a number of Christian friends at work and here are some of the answers that they shared.

'I am not confident enough to speak to people about Jesus because I don't know the Bible well enough. What will I do if they ask a challenging question?'

'Sometimes I'm afraid to share my faith with other people because I am worried that they'll think I'm a hypocrite. I'm not the best Christian in the world. I'm only just learning how to serve Jesus. I must learn a lot more before I can try to teach others.'

'I never know what to say to people! How do you start a conversation about Jesus with someone you don't know all that well? No, I'm just too afraid that they'll laugh at me.'

'I've tried to share my faith in Jesus with other people, but we always seem to end up arguing about what I believe, or things that Christians and the church do wrong. Even when I win the arguments the other person never seems to be convinced enough to make a commitment to Jesus.'

I'm sure that you could list your own reasons for not witnessing to the people around you about Jesus and his love. It was interesting to hear how many of the people I spoke to expressed some measure of guilt because they were not obeying Christ's command to 'go into all the world' to make disciples (Matt 28:19, NKJV). One particular person even expressed the fear that Jesus would disown him because of what is written in Matthew 10:33, 'But whoever disowns me before men, I will disown him before my Father in heaven.' Of course this particular verse means something different when one reads it in the context of Matthew 10 as a whole, which is about persecution for the faith in Jesus, something that the early Christians knew all too well! Jesus was preparing his disciples for the hardships to come.

Very few Christians in the western world face anything nearly as dangerous and challenging as those first disciples – yet for some reason we are still afraid to witness to our faith.

The early Christians who gave their lives for their faith in Jesus were known as 'witnesses'. In Greek they were called *marturion*, from which we get our English word 'martyr'. Regardless of the time in history and the place on the planet, a true witness (or testimony) for Jesus is going to be costly! You can be assured of this – it cost Jesus his life in order to witness to his love for you, therefore it is certain to cost you something to effectively witness to your love for Him!

> *The early Christians who gave their lives for their faith in Jesus were known as 'witnesses'. In Greek they were called marturion, from which we get our English word 'martyr'.*

However, that being said, none of the reasons given above should stop you from witnessing to Jesus' love for you and for the people around you. You certainly do not need to be a theologian or a Biblical scholar in order to testify to Jesus' love. You also don't necessarily have to be an extrovert who can strike up a conversation with anybody, in order to share Christ's love with others.

We have been truly blessed to have discovered a Biblical model for sharing Christ's love with our employees, our clients, our families and our friends! And best of all, this model can be used by just about any person of any age to reach people with the love of Christ.

## Getting to Grips with Evangelism

What do you think of when you hear the words 'evangelism' and 'evangelist'? Most of us tend to think of evangelism as a form of 'preaching' where one shares truths about God's love for people and the world with individuals or groups. When we think of an evangelist we tend to think of people like Billy Graham, preaching to massive crowds of eager listeners.

This is certainly one perspective on evangelism and evangelists. However, one of the clearest and most accessible images of evangelism is the one that Jesus Himself taught his disciples when He sent them out into the world to witness to his love for the first time. You will find this remarkable model of evangelism in Luke 10:5–9.

You may be surprised to see how simple, yet different, Jesus' model of evangelism is when you compare it to many of the more popular models that are used today.

The Greek word used in the Bible, from which we get our English word 'evangelism' is the verb *euangelizo* which means to bring 'good news'. The more popular understanding of 'preaching the good news' comes from another Greek word, *kerusso*, which means 'to proclaim' or 'to preach'. This second understanding of 'preaching the good news' has become an almost exclusive approach to evangelism in much of the church. There is little doubt that it can be effective in many situations. However, it is also certain that it is not always the most effective or appropriate means of introducing people to the love and transforming power of Jesus.

*When last did you hear the Gospel preached with passion, conviction and in a manner that made accepting Jesus a truly attractive proposition?*

There are many reasons why preaching and proclaiming the good news do not always work. Sometimes people's hearts have become so hardened against the good news that they simply will not listen to what you have to say. I have also encountered many people who are not open to having a conversation about God's love – instead they would prefer to argue about some theological or Biblical point with which they do not agree. Another challenge in contemporary society is the difficulty of 'competing truths'. Magazines, television programs, movie stars and even politicians often present ideas that are contrary to the Gospel of Jesus. With the aid of flashy media campaigns and the backing of communication experts it is not uncommon for people to feel confused and conflicted about the truth! This leads me to a final point that I would like to make in this regard. While preaching the Gospel does work when it is done with passion, conviction and skill, there are very few Christians, and even fewer churches, that can present the Gospel in a compelling, convincing and attractive manner. Just think about the church services that you have visited in the last number of months – if a person was looking for answers in life, searching for forgiveness, salvation, and God's love, would they have found it in a clear and powerful way in those services? When I thought about this question I had to admit that we are not all that great at proclaiming the good news of Christ's saving and transforming love.

So, what is the solution? In the next section of this chapter I will introduce a method of bringing the love of Jesus to people. This method has had powerful and lasting results in our context. Graham and I first learnt about this approach to evangelism when we read Ed Silvoso's book *Prayer Evangelism* (Regal books, 2000).

# Luke 10 Transformation

As a pastor I had worked out a pretty clear strategy for obeying the command to '... go and make disciples of all nations, baptising them in the name of the Father and of the Son and of the Holy Spirit, and teaching them to obey everything I have commanded you' (Matt 28:19–20).

Firstly, I did my best to prepare and deliver the best sermons I could. I would read the Bible earnestly, spend hours in prayer, get to know the people I would be preaching to, and then put together a great message. On Sunday I would preach with all my heart! In an ideal world hundreds of people would come to church and all of them would respond to my sermon! But the reality was never as grand as that – in fact, most Sundays I preached to the same faithful followers of Christ. There were very few people 'walking in off the street' searching for the truth! On a good Sunday ten or fifteen of the five hundred worshippers would respond to the message by seeking prayer, ministry, or counsel. This is not a great success rate! Once people had responded to the message we would then do our best to motivate them to join some kind of community or group (a Bible study, an Alpha course, a fellowship or prayer group and so on). It was my desire and intention that groups such as these would form their participants for loving and faithful service in Christ. Finally, once people had proven themselves to be mature in their faith and dependable in their witness and ministry in the church, we would normally bring them into the leadership of the church where they would have the blessing and joy to shape the life and work of our church.

If I am honest, this was not a very effective or efficient system! While I had a fair number of people sitting in the pews on Sunday, our church was not having an incredible impact upon our surrounding community. I think it would be fair to say that this model is the norm in most churches.

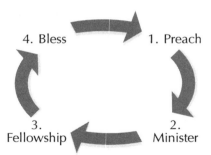

However, when you look at Jesus' model in Luke 10 you will see that Jesus encourages his disciples to start from the other end.

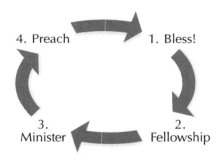

- Jesus says we should start by *blessing* the people we encounter, 'When you enter a house, first say, 'Peace to this house' (Luke 10:5). Everybody longs to experience blessing, acceptance and love. This is something that is so simple and easy to do – sometimes it just involves a sincere compliment, or perhaps a practical act of caring (like helping a co-worker to reach a deadline). Very few people can resist genuine and sincere blessing from others. Peace is not only a physical state, you can also bless a person by offering to pray for him. I have even blessed people by praying for them without their knowing it!

*Speak to God about the lost before speaking to the lost about God.*

— ED SILVOSO

- Next, Jesus encourages us to build *relationships* with people, 'Stay in that house, eating and drinking whatever they give you …' (Luke 10:7). I have made a habit of cultivating friendships with people who don't know the Lord. I belong to a cycling club of people where most of the guys don't yet know Jesus. I engage in MBWA at work each day (I say it is better than an MBA, it is Management By Walking Around). I take just five minutes to pop my head into a few offices each day to say 'Hi' to the people who work in our company. I make a point of getting to know their names and the names of their spouses and children, and of hearing about their interests, challenges and joys. In these interactions I keep two simple principles in mind. Firstly, I treat each person as special (see Philippians 2:5–7). Secondly, I always do my best to share the fruit of love with them (see Matthew 7:16). God loves the people I encounter and I want to do my best to show them that they are loved!

> *People don't care how much you know until*
> *they know how much you care*
>
> – JOHN C. MAXWELL

- Thirdly, Jesus says that once we have blessed people and built friendships with them, we should *minister to their needs*, '… heal the sick who are there…' (Luke 10:9). This is the most amazing step in this simple process. I have come to discover that when people have experienced what it is to be blessed, and trust you because you have built a real relationship with them, they suddenly start opening up. They start asking questions about my faith, 'Why are you so calm when things go wrong?' or 'Why is it that you seem to cope so much better with conflict than other people?' However, even more important than that, they frequently ask for help and prayer. I have prayed for so many colleagues, friends and staff members over the years simply because they feel they can trust me and they know that it is my desire to bless them. One further encouragement that I would offer you on this point, is to try and respond to people's 'felt needs' first. Hardship, struggle, stress and pain have a tendency to cause people to adopt a narrow focus. For example, the Salvation Army has the approach of offering people soup, soap and then salvation. They know that a person who is hungry and dirty would be less likely to respond to an invitation to salvation than someone who felt fed and cared for, and so their first step in sharing the Gospel is to feed people and care for their practical needs before they try to address their spiritual needs.

- Finally, Jesus ends up where we most often start – *preaching and teaching*, '… tell them, "The kingdom of God is near you"' (Luke 10:9). In 1 Peter 3:15 we get this very sound advice, 'Always be prepared to give an answer to everyone who asks you to give the reason for the hope that you have. But do this with gentleness and respect …' When a person's need is met you will have a golden opportunity to share the good news with him. When a prayer is answered, or a person finds the help that he needs, you can gently tell him about God's power and provision. My experience is that the most effective preaching that you can do is to testify about something that God has done for you. Or help the person to recognise what God is doing for him. In doing this you are helping him to understand the principles of God's kingdom.
- There are many wonderful resources that can help you to apply this Biblical method of evangelism effectively. In particular we have used the 'Luke 10 Transformation' material by Willem Joubert and 'Prayer Evangelism' by Ed Silvoso.

## Luke 10 Transformation
## – Two Testimonies

We have experienced the effectiveness of this method in many different ways. One of the great testimonies of this method came during the economic downturn of 2009. The construction and development industry was particularly hard hit by the recession since banks became very cautious about granting loans to customers. However, since Graham had clearly understood the principles of prayer evangelism and Luke 10 Transformation, we experienced a wonderful miracle. Graham had built strong relationships with many clients and the owners and CEOs of other construction and development companies over the years. Moreover, we frequently pray for our industry. Since our goal is to be used by God to 'Transform the lives of Africans through infrastructure development' we know that we need others to partner in the process of building houses, roads, schools and so forth. So, step one, blessing, and step two, fellowship, were an ongoing focus for Graham and our team. However, when the economic situation began to place severe pressure on other players in the market God began to give Graham and others in our company many wonderful opportunities to practise the principles of the Luke 10 Transformation.

We were fortunate to weather the economic storms and even showed some growth as a result of commitment, dedication, ethics and Christlike values in our work. Soon Graham was getting phone calls and meeting requests from various friends in other companies. As each one came, he would minister to them – encouraging them from Scripture, praying for them and their companies, and even offering sound business advice. But, he would not leave it at step three, to minister, he would always move to the final step, which is to preach the good news. I have personally witnessed many senior business people come closer to God as Graham challenged them to come clean in their business dealings. He has shared how God honours hard work and honesty (see Proverbs 11:1). And so, through a simple process of blessing, be-friending, ministering and proclaiming, God has used Graham to impact an industry and a nation.

You may not have the influence and authority that Graham has. However, it is important to recognise that God wants to use you to share his love with the people you encounter each day. When I moved into my home in Cape Town I asked the Lord to show me what he wanted me to do in my suburb. The Lord challenged me to minister to a local petrol filling station! Can you imagine? Well, after some wres-tling I obeyed his command and started practising the Luke 10 Transformation method. Firstly, I prayed that God would bless and protect the business and all the people who worked there. But I knew that the most practical blessing I could give this filling station was to do my best to only fill my car there and to get my friends to do the same – businesses are blessed when they make money! Next, whenever I went to get fuel or buy something at the shop I would get to know each one of the staff members. At first they were a little cautious, but they soon came to know and trust me. I learnt all their names, as well as the names of their spouses and children. After a few months of blessing them without them knowing and of build-ing relationships with the staff I slowly started creating opportunities for ministry. When I asked a staff member how his family was one day, he told me that one of his children was ill. So, I asked him if I could pray with him. Because he knew me he said okay. So we prayed. I kept checking back with him and even offered to get some medicine for his child. He was astounded! It wasn't long before he approached me one day to ask why I was being kind to him and his colleagues – that was the moment to preach. I simply told him how much God loves him, and that God had told me that my job was to show him how much God loved him. That was enough for him to accept Jesus as his Savior! Now I am teaching him to use the Luke 10 Transformation approach to reach the people who come to the filling station each day.

God can achieve so much for his kingdom if we are just willing to be used by Him!

## Points to Ponder

I hope that you have seen that there is an amazing opportunity for you to share Jesus' love in a simple, non-threatening way, every day? All it takes is some commitment in prayer and a willingness to let God use you to show his love. Isn't it amazing to think that God wants to use people like you and me to transform the world? What a privilege!

- Who does God put you into contact with regularly? It may be a person you know, or someone you meet occasionally at work or in your community (like our garage attendants). Start praying that God will bless these people and their families. Make a short list of people that you can pray for every day. I use our company 'telephone list' as a guide. Because we have so many employees I try to pray for a few of them each day by name, so that all the people I work with are prayed for by name every week. As you are praying for them, ask God to show you how you can bless them in a practical and tangible manner.
- Next, who are the people that God would want you to build stronger, more trusting relationships with? Remember, people don't care what you know until they know how much you care! You may need to consider doing something extra (for example, I joined a cycling club) in order to build relationships with the people who do not know Jesus. You will very quickly discover that opportunities such as these can be perfect for sharing God's love with people who do not know Him yet! Make a commitment to grow closer to two or three people this month. Invest time and energy in them and win their friendship for Christ.
- If you think about the people around you, what are their most pressing 'felt needs'? Pray and ask God to show you how you can minister to them practically. Occasionally, I take a cup of coffee to one of our busiest secretaries. I always try to set aside a few minutes a day to follow up on people that I know are having a rough time. There are so many practical things that you can do, like leaving someone a note, or blessing them with a gift for their children, or passing on a good book.
- Finally, what testimony do you have that tells of an answered prayer or God's provision? If it is someone else's story, get their permission to share it with

some others. It is always helpful to remember a few testimonies that you can use to encourage and challenge other towards faith.

Questions for discussion

- Please read Luke 10:2–9 again slowly. What do you notice as you read the text? Is there anything in particular that God may be saying to you through this passage of Scripture?
- What obstacles do you experience to evangelism? Please list a few items that stop you from sharing your faith with others.
- How did you come to hear about Jesus and how did you find out about his love?
- Can you list the four steps of the Luke 10 Transformation? Memorising these steps will help you to become more effective in reaching others with Jesus' love.
- What differences can you see between this approach to evangelism and some of the traditional approaches to evangelism? Is there anything in this approach that you will need to learn to do in order to allow God to use you most effectively?
- Please suggest people among whom you can apply the steps of the Luke 10 Transformation in your workplace. Remember to ensure that your steps in addressing their 'felt needs' are practical and tangible.
- Take some time to commit yourselves to one person or project that you can engage using the Luke 10 Transformation model. Please pray for one another and commit yourselves to this task in prayer. Ask God to give you the love, time, commitment and resources that you need to complete this task to his glory.

To clasp the hands in prayer is the beginning of an uprising!

– Karl Barth

The prayer of a person living right with God is something
powerful to be reckoned with. Elijah, for instance, human just like us, prayed hard that it wouldn't rain,
and it didn't – not a drop for three and a half years. Then he prayed that it would rain, and it did.
The showers came and everything started growing again.

– James 5:16–18 (The Message)

# 9

## ON SITE WITH INSIGHT:

## Prayers that Change the World

I f you have not yet begun to see the big breakthroughs you long for in your life, it is likely that you are not praying as you should be. Prayer is one of the most powerful tools that any marketplace minister can draw on to see change and transformation come to pass. Why? Because prayer connects you to the source of all change and power – the almighty God! God is the one who transforms the impossible into the possible (see Mattew 19:26), it is God who brings forth water in the desert (see Isaiah 48:21), it is God who makes a way in the wilderness (see Isaiah 43:19, KJV), it is God who creates and recreates by the power of his voice (see Genesis 1:3–27), it is God who created you and gave you your reason for living – it is God.

## A Builder in Prayer?

Graham is the most unlikely person to have been called to prayer! I have often heard him tell the story of God instructing him to call together all the Christians in the city of Cape Town 'for a day of repentance and prayer'. With a chuckle in his voice Graham always asks, 'Lord, why prayer? Why not ask me to build houses for the poor? Or orphanages and hospitals?'

Graham is quite right! His gifting, training, abilities and life's experience do suggest that he would be far better at building houses and buildings than mobilising people for prayer. However, it took the practical determination of a businessman, a person who understands 'Gantt diagrams' and 'critical pathways', who knows how to overcome challenges and obstacles, who works with determination towards a single goal, to figure out how to get every country on earth to respond to the challenge of 2 Chronicles 7:14 '… if my people, who are called by my name, will humble themselves and pray and seek my face and turn from their wicked ways, then will I hear from heaven and will forgive their sin and will heal their land'. In 2009 Christians from every country on earth participated in the ninth Global Day of Prayer on

Pentecost Sunday. Hundreds of millions of people all over the world rose to the challenge to 'stand in the gap' for their towns, cities and nations (see Ezekiel 22:30).

This prayer movement has been called the largest single prayer gathering in all recorded history, and God chose to use a businessman from the continent of Africa to birth it.

I have since come to understand the kingdom principle that this incredible move of God teaches us: in God's kingdom it is not ability, but availability, that counts. God uses the most unlikely people to do the most extraordinary things! In doing so, no one but God can claim the glory! Graham is the first to acknowledge that it is neither his ability, nor his skill, nor even the work of a committee or a team that has achieved this incredible miracle. It is only God and God's power that spread the Global Day of Prayer across the earth.

> *In God's kingdom it is not ability, but availability, that counts. God uses the most unlikely people to do the most extraordinary things! In doing so, no one but God can claim the glory!*

Paul makes this same point when he says, 'But God chose the foolish things of the world to shame the wise; God chose the weak things of the world to shame the strong' (1 Cor 1:27).

By choosing a construction worker to birth the world's largest prayer movement God showed that it is his power that achieves great things. The great news is that God wants to do the same with you and through you.

## Are we all Intercessors?

At the start of this chapter I said that if you have not yet begun to see the big breakthroughs in your life, it is likely that you are not praying as you should. This is quite a controversial statement, but I believe it is true. Many Christians only pay lip-service to prayer. It only forms a very small part of our daily lives, and a very small part of our ministry.

I have frequently heard marketplace ministers commenting 'Prayer is not my calling'. It is almost as if they use this phrase as a justification for not engaging in deep, committed and intense prayer. Every Christian is called to prayer! Our sincere and intimate engagement with God around our lives is not as a result of a calling to prayer.

Rather, prayer is an expected part of every Christian's relationship with God. Paul says clearly 'Be joyful always; *pray continually*; give thanks in all circumstances, for *this is God's will for you* in Christ Jesus' (1 Thes 5:16–18, NIV, *emphasis added*). It is God's will that we should pray continually. The Greek word used here literally means that we should always be in prayer; that we should pray without ceasing.

---

*Prayer is not a calling, it is a lifestyle.*

---

I am pleased to say that Graham is a man of prayer. He spends hours each week in prayer. He prays alone in his office in the mornings, and throughout the day you will often find him praying with staff members, praying at tough stages during meetings, visiting projects to pray on the land and gathering with other Christians to pray about issues in our business, our city and our nation.

I do agree, however, that there are certain people who have a *specific calling* to bring people and issues before God in an intentional, passionate and determined manner – these people are most frequently called intercessors. While there are some who are called to this ministry as their primary function, it is a ministry that all Christians share in.

'I urge, then, first of all, that requests, prayers, intercession and thanksgiving be made for everyone – for kings and all those in authority, that we may live peaceful and quiet lives in all godliness and holiness. This is good, and pleases God our Savior, who wants all men to be saved and to come to a knowledge of the truth' (1 Tim 2:1–4).

So, every Christian parent should be bringing their children before God. Every Christian should be praying for their leaders and those in authority. In fact, 1 Timothy 2:1 says that prayers and intercession should be made 'for everyone'.

Let us consider it from a different vantage point. Just because some Christians are called to preach does not mean that all Christians are not expected to share their faith with others. It is not the activity that differs (prayer, preaching, hospitality, leadership and so forth) but the manner in which it is approached.

In the most basic sense an intercessor is someone who intercedes on behalf of a particular person or situation. The intercessor is expected to represent someone else in pleading their case before God.

In the Old Testament the priests would come before God to represent the people, making sacrifices for their sins and asking for God's mercy and help in times of hardship and struggle. In the New Testament, however, we read that every believer is a 'priest' (see 1 Peter 2:5, 9).

Thus, while some may be called to the ministry of intercession, we are all intercessors! If you are a Christian you are expected to pray for the people, places and situations that you encounter each day. Can you imagine how powerful it would be if every business, every school, every hospital and every home had people who were intently bringing them before God in prayer? Tapping into that power would transform the spiritual climate of a city and make it ripe for transformation!

## Power in Prayer

A short while after Graham was saved in 1999 he began to realise just how powerful prayer is, and how necessary it was to get people praying for him and the things God had called him to do. At that time God brought two very special friends across Graham's path, namely Barbara Cilliers and AyJay Jaantjies, both of whom have been called to the ministry of intercession.

Paul writes about Epaphras who was an intercessor for the church in Colosse, saying, 'He is always wrestling in prayer for you, that you may stand firm in all the will of God, mature and fully assured' (Col 4:12).

Barbara and AyJay immediately started 'wrestling in prayer' for Graham so that he would 'stand firm in all the will of God, mature and fully assured'. People such as Barbara and AyJay are an invaluable gift to the marketplace minister! I have also come to experience the blessing of Barbara and AyJay's prayers for my ministry and family. I have so many testimonies that I could share of how I asked them to intercede for me before the Lord (bringing my case before the Lord) for tough meetings, difficult decisions, courage to do what is right, difficult business dealings, insight and revelation, physical healing … The list could go on and on! By asking them to pray for me I am not absolved of my responsibility to pray, but I do have the assurance of knowing that there are some people who are continually bringing my situation before God as I go about the task of finding solutions to problems, taking risks to achieve new goals and so on.

In general there are three kinds of intercessors and intercessory prayer groupings that we have used in the Power Group:

- Firstly, there are those who are *general prayers*. These are faithful people who have the company and the staff at heart! They love the Lord and they know that God has a special plan for the Power Group. We have a number of prayers who work on our staff (for example we have a prayer room on our head office campus, and a number of our staff, led by one of our staff members Erica, gathers each day between 9:00–9:30 to share prayer requests and pray for the company, the staff, the leadership and any other prayer-related matters). There are other people who pray for our company elsewhere in the country and the world. We send messages through to these people, sharing our 'pressure points', asking them to stand with us on certain issues and encouraging them to intercede for us in a general sense. While we will share news of the outcome of their prayers, we will seldom hear direct messages back from them. This group is not a 'listening' group as such.

- Secondly, we have a group called *intercessors*. This is a smaller, closer group of people who have been called to the ministry of intercession and many of them have been called to pray specifically for the Power Group of companies, for Graham or for myself. At 'Eagle's Rising', a local ministry in Somerset West, we have a group of about thirty students who spend extended time in prayer for our company and our staff. Together with them there is another group of about eight people who gather weekly to pray for us and what we are involved in. What is different about this group, in comparison to the group above, is that they spend much more time praying specifically for us. They require quite specific and detailed information (for example what exact projects are we struggling with, what clients are we meeting, what do we specifically hope to achieve in a meeting, what do we want specific guidance or answers on from God and so forth.) This group is also a group that listens to God for guidance, revelation, warnings and specific words of knowledge.

- Thirdly, we have a group of *inner circle intercessors*. This group is very small. My inner circle only has three people in it: Barbara, AyJay and Estelle Evans. These trusted friends have journeyed with us for many years. They will often have information that very few other people will have access to. They know our families personally, will frequently be present at important meetings or events and sometimes even travel with us. This group has access to our appointment book and can see where we are going and who we are seeing. I make a point of sharing as much information as possible with this group. They often spend hours bringing us, as well as the Power Group, before the Lord. They will also wait upon God for specific instruction and revelation and they will often engage in spiritual warfare on our behalf.

It is critical that you get as many people as possible praying for you and your ministry.

---

*It is critical that you get as many people as possible praying for you and your work and ministry.*

---

I would encourage you to ask God to bring the right people across your path. As God introduces you to people, or you build friendships with people, consider which level of intercession you would like to ask of them. Some would be general prayers, some may be more specific intercessors and others will form part of your inner circle of prayer, guidance and protection.

## Some Examples of 'Power in Prayer'

Since we understand that God wants to be a part of everything that we are doing in the company and we acknowledge that we can do nothing without God, we do a number of specific things with prayer in the Power Group.

- Firstly, we produce a 'Power in Prayer' newsletter in our company that shares general news about the company, asks for prayer for people who have lost loved ones, members of our staff who are ill, and gives thanks for special breakthroughs in our business, or special celebrations in our community (such as weddings, births, birthdays and so on).
- Secondly, we have an internal mailing system that distributes urgent prayer requests throughout the whole company. For example, if someone is injured, or there is a sudden death, we can mobilise many people for prayer just by sending out an email to all of our employees. We have a staff member, Antoinette, who takes care of this responsibility for us. You may not be allowed to go as wide as sending an email to all the employees in your company, but do your best to mobilise a trusted few at least. Every prayer counts!
- Thirdly, I have taken the responsibility of praying for each of our staff by name at least once a month. Together with our intercessors I pray specifically for our senior management, their families and their teams. I will often just drop them a personal email or text message to let them know that I am praying for them, or just drop by their office for a minute to see if there is anything specific they want me to pray for. It is amazing what a response this simple little action illicits; both

in answer to prayer, and in building relationships with the senior staff.

- Fourthly, we frequently mobilise specific prayer for specific issues, places or people. One of the great testimonies that we have in this regard is one of our commercial developments, Saxenberg Park. While we were busy laying out the roads and developing the infrastructure for this office park we invited our intercessors to come and pray on the grounds. We asked them to dedicate the land to God and ask God to bless all the buildings that would be built there, to protect those who would establish factories and offices in the park, and to break off any evil that may have been done on the land in the past, or may try to gain entry to the land in the future. They walked the land, anointed it with oil as a sign of dedication to Christ and they prayed for the whole development. That development sold faster than any other development we had done before it! It is still a wonderful model in the industry. We have many such testimonies. For example, we recently built thousands of affordable houses for the local government. Before we handed over the homes to the minister we invited our intercessory teams to pray in each home! Each home was dedicated to Christ, the family that would move into the home was brought before the Lord in prayer and the community as a whole was prayed for. I also schedule time to visit our teams who are working out on the roads or on various sites across the country. I pray on the roads that we are constructing, asking God to bless and protect those who will drive there. I ask God to protect our workforce and to give us a strong witness as people see our 'Unashamedly Ethical' or 'Kingdom developers' signboards along the roads.
- Fifthly, some of our intercessors (mainly members of our staff who have felt a calling to intercede and have been trained to do so) and I sit in on our company's meetings to pray for the company, the leadership and the issues we are discussing and dealing with. For example, I attend our 'procurement' meetings every two weeks. I open the meeting in prayer and then take careful notes to see where our teams are working, what challenges they are facing, where we need more work and so forth. I then feed this information through to our intercessory teams for prayer. I also frequently attend the executive committee and senior management meetings to offer prayer support and to listen for the Lord's guidance and input on our company's strategic direction.
- Finally, we engage in *prayer evangelism*. I have devoted the whole of Chapter 8 to this subject, so I am not going to discuss it here.

In the past we have had a full-time intercessor on the company staff. In our case this was a sensible thing to do since we have a prayer room for our employees and we have a lot of prayer-directed activity that requires leadership and attention. It is important that the person who occupies this position is called to intercession and is trusted by the senior Christian staff. We were blessed with the lady who filled this role for us and when she was called into ministry with her husband, we were sad to lose her.

On a final note about intercessors, there are a few points that I would like to make about this critical ministry in your company or marketplace ministry.

- Prayer is critical, it connects you with God who has the power to do all things. As such, prayer should be every Christian's ministry, not just the task of some people who feel called to this specific ministry. Therefore do your best to get as many people as possible to exercise their responsibility to pray!
- Intercessors should not be viewed as a 'oracles'. If you are in leadership in your company God will expect you to gather all the information you can and then make an informed decision and bear responsibility for it. Ask your intercessors for their guidance, receive the information and consider it prayerfully and responsibly. But ultimately you have to make the decisions yourself about what God wants you to do. It is always wise to seek multiple confirmations of a specific word, vision or prophecy before acting upon it. Also, be sure to weigh all input against the teachings of the Bible. Graham will frequently check things with me as a pastor, simply because I have spent years reading and studying the Scriptures, and can fairly easily discern when something is not entirely trustworthy.
- Maintaining a healthy relationship with intercessors takes time and effort. It will take time and discernment to work out who you can trust  and at what level of intercession you can utilise them. In our case, it requires careful management of communication to the people who pray for us, and it also requires receiving feedback from them to inform our decisions and choices. In the end, however, we would not have it any other way! Every hour spent on prayer is rewarded one hundred times over when we find ourselves closer to God's will, more obedient and sustained for the tasks God is giving us.
- Finally, intercession is needed at every level of the marketplace. In Chapter 10, I tell Eleanor's story – even if you are not the boss, Eleanor's story reminds us that every person's prayers carry equal weight to transform his or her work life

and workplace! God used Eleanor and some other members of staff in the Power Group to start an incredible transformation process that eventually led to Graham's conversion, some very significant changes in the company and ultimately to the birth of the Global Day of Prayer. God wants to use you where you are to make a massive difference! So, I want to encourage you to start interceding today!

---

*God wants to use you where you are to make a massive difference!*
*So, I want to encourage you to start interceding today!*

---

## Points to Ponder

- We read in James 5:16 that 'The prayer of a righteous man is powerful and effective' (NIV). What proportion of your time do you spend praying specifically for your workplace and the people that you work with? It may just be that God is longing to reveal a whole treasure trove of blessings to you, if you would just take the time to intercede for your workplace.
- I have come to discover that negativity is an antidote to faith. I so frequently hear people complaining about situations that they have not even bothered to pray about! What situation, or person, in your work life bothers you most? I want to encourage you to intercede for that person or situation and get a few other trusted intercessors to stand with you in prayer. You will see how amazingly God can change people and situations as you pray about them. If it is important to you, please make a sacrificial commitment to intercede for the person or situation. Take at least fifteen to thirty minutes a day to pray just for that person or issue. Commit to do this for a month. Keep a little journal of what you pray about and any answers to prayer, revelations, verses from Scripture, or insights that come through during that period.
- What is the most impossible thing in your work life at the moment? Remember that God often wants to use the impossible things in life to show his power (like using a construction guy to mobilize millions of people for prayer)! Make a note of this 'huge challenge' and start to cultivate the discipline of asking God to show you how to achieve the impossible under God's guidance, with God's power!
- As the German theologian Karl Barth said, 'To clasp the hands in prayer is the beginning of an uprising!'

Questions for Group Discussion

- In this chapter we showed that God has called each of us to be an intercessor (at some level). What level has God called you to?
- How important is prayer in your work life at the moment?
- What hindrances to prayer do you face?
- What could you do in order to motivate yourself and others to pray more intentionally for your work life and your workplace?
- Please take some time to make a list of 'prayer needs' among your group members. I would suggest that you focus on at least the following areas – spiritual growth and each member's relationship with Christ, each member's family and family life, any personal struggles or challenges and each member's work life and marketplace ministry.

It is not the critic who counts; not the man who points out
how the strong man stumbles, or where the doer of deeds could have done better. The credit
belongs to the man who is actually in the arena … who, at best, knows in the end the triumph
of great achievements, and who, at worst, if he fails, at least fails while daring greatly. So that his
place will never be with those cold, timid souls who know neither victory nor defeat.

– Theodore Roosevelt

'… I am with you always, to the very end of the age.'
– Matthew 28:20

'With man this is impossible, but not with God;
all things are possible with God.'
– Mark 10:27

# 10

## WHAT IF I AM NOT THE BOSS?

### Eleanor's Story

One of the more common questions that I am asked when I tell people about Graham's courage and commitment to ministry in the marketplace is, 'That's great for Graham! But what could I possibly do? You see, I'm not the boss!' The reality is, of course, that most people are not in positions to decide to change the policies of their company by calling together the leadership. Most of us do not have the freedom to decide how we will spend our time in the workplace. In fact, if I have to be honest, when I speak to most ordinary working people they do not have much confidence in their ability to have a significant impact on their workplace and transform it for Jesus.

In working with Graham in the Power Group I have come to see, however, that no matter what level of the company you work at (whether you are the chairman of the board, like Graham, or someone who works in the office) there will always be challenges and obstacles to bringing Jesus' love to bear on the people and systems you encounter!

---

*It is a mistake to think that simply having a different position in your company will make witnessing for Jesus and ministering to others any easier.*

---

## A Pattern for Ministry in the Marketplace

I have discovered that in order to be used by God to bring about an amazing change we need a few simple, yet necessary, things to happen in our lives. As I have studied the lives of many, many people who have made an impact on the people in their sphere of influence and have brought them nearer to Christ, these elements have almost always been present. It does not matter what position you occupy in your company, what title you hold, or how much you earn, if you can get these few points right you will start to see things change around you and you will begin to feel the immeasurable joy of living every moment of your life as God intended it to be lived! You may feel that it is impossible to achieve something truly great for God where you are. Above the door of one of the dining halls at the University of Edinburgh it says the following:'When God is going to do something wonderful, He chooses a difficulty. When He is going to do something very wonderful, He chooses an impossibility!'

Here are a few points you will need to get in place so that God can work with you and through you in your work life:

*Firstly*, you will have to decide that your primary reason for living is to honour Jesus. As we discussed in the first three chapters of this book, living for Jesus and his will is the only thing that will ever bring you true peace, true blessing and true reward – God made you to live for Him. There is no position, salary or possession that can replace this truth. Living for Jesus is a daily choice! It takes courage to face people you may not like, or tasks that wear you down and say, 'Lord, I'm doing this for You! I will go where you send me and do what you give me to do with passion, commitment and love!' Choosing to live your life for Jesus almost certainly means that you will have to choose not to live for some other things (such as simply living for your own desire and happiness, or living for the acceptance of certain people, or a measure of worldly acclaim). God's way is good – it is the way of true life (see John 3:15–17; John 10:10).

*Secondly*, we have already seen that God uses love to transform people and situations. In Chapter 8 we showed how asking God to help you love the people around you in practical and simple ways can change even the toughest people, or the most difficult situations, into opportunities for God's Spirit to work in power and love! Once again this step begins with you. You have to choose to love the people and the place where God has placed you to work. It is seldom easy to love people and places that do not necessarily want your love. However, persistent and consistent love is God's nature; that is how God loves the world! The Bible says it so clearly when Paul writes that, 'But God demonstrates his own love for us in this: While we were still sinners, Christ died for us' (Rom 5:8). Jesus' parable of the Prodigal Son illustrates this principle even more clearly. God is unrelenting in his love for you and the people who work and live around you! God never gives up, God never tires of loving you, God is always trying to find new and creative ways to show you how special and significant you are to Him. Listen to how Paul describes Godly love, 'It always protects, always trusts, always hopes, always perseveres. Love never fails …' (1 Cor 13:7–8a). It may take some time to cultivate this kind of Godly love for your colleagues and your workplace, but when it comes it is a force that cannot be stopped! It is more powerful than any position or title that you could ever hold. It is irresistible to even the hardest of hearts!

---

*It may take some time to cultivate this kind of Godly love for your colleagues and your workplace, but when it comes it is a force that cannot be stopped!*

---

*Thirdly*, you will need the courage to act. If your life belongs to Jesus and you truly love the people among whom Jesus places you, then it will soon become impossible not to act upon that love! Just like a parent responds naturally to one of his or her children who is hurt or lost, you will soon find that it becomes the most natural thing to respond to the needs and questions of those people you encounter during your day. If your love and obedience do not lead to action then you need to go back to the drawing-board! 'But someone will say, "You have faith; I have deeds." Show me your faith without deeds, and I will show you my faith by what I do' (Jas 2:18). An appropriate action is far more powerful than a creative sermon! The right words of encouragement at the right moment, or a simple little act of help and service can have a far greater impact on someone than the most eloquent and theologically astute sermon in the world! When I think about some of the most powerful things that have happened in my life, they have been simple things – like the friend who came to help me one early morning when my car would not start. Or the colleague who could see that I was nearing the end of my tether. Instead of offering me advice, he simply brought me a cup of coffee and a smile. When God creates an opportunity for you to act, no matter how small it is, have the courage to do something! More things have been achieved in the world by small, simple acts of kindness than by massive campaigns.

> *'Everybody is afraid! The difference between people who succeed and those who fail, is that the successful have learnt to overcome their fears and live life anyway! What is better, to be afraid and try, or simply to be afraid?'*
>
> — BRIAN TRACY

*Finally*, it is important to start with what you can do, and not to get tripped up by the things that are out of your reach. Because God wants you to find blessing and joy in your life, and to use your life to bring blessing and joy to others, God is pleased when you do what you can! I think of it a bit like a parent thinks about his young child. My son is only four years old. I have incredible dreams for him as he grows older and learns to do more and more complex and marvellous things. However, for now I only require him to do what he can do for his age and to do it to the best of his ability – that is enough! I am pleased when he is a great four-year-old! I have often found myself paralysed by the size of a looming task. How can I possibly bring every person in my company to Jesus? How can I change the policies of my company or industry to reflect the values of God's kingdom? However, what Jesus requires of me is to start with what I can change, and with the people on whose lives I can have an impact! You will be amazed at how quickly God increases his favour and starts trusting you with more! Do you remember Jesus' parable of the talents? 'Well done, good and faithful servant! You have been faithful with a few things; I will put you in charge of many things. Come and share your master's happiness!' (Matt 25:21).

The pattern is simple: obedience, love, action and focus. If you can start to get these four things in order today you will be able to measure the results of change in your work life in just a few weeks or months.

## Eleanor's Story

If you still need a little more convincing about how God uses ordinary people to do extraordinary things, then read on just a little bit more. You see, long before I started working with Graham, and long before Graham came to know Jesus and started to have an impact on his company and the world through his obedience, there was a lady named Eleanor.

Eleanor started working as a secretary at the Power Group of companies many years ago. Her greatest distinction is that she loves the Lord passionately! I have seldom met someone who is so sincere and committed to Christ as she is. Eleanor was not called to be a pastor of a church and she also did not hold a senior position in the company when she started working here. However, she was certain that God is powerful enough to change any situation and that God could use her obedience, commitment and love to transform her company and her bosses to serve Him! For Eleanor prayer was the key to seeing change happen in the Power Group.

And so, after there had been some struggles at work and in her personal life, she started praying for changes in both her personal life, as well as her company and her bosses. Years before Graham knew the Lord, Eleanor was interceding for him and the other leadership of the company.

That is the wonderful thing about prayer – even Graham wasn't aware that she was standing in the gap for him and for our company (see Ezekiel 22:30), but because of her obedience God started to change things at Power!

Eleanor would pray for each of her bosses by name and eventually she had a small group of Christians in the company who joined her in praying for their bosses and for our company as a whole. They went as far as taking small vials of anointing oil and anointing the desks and the doors of the people they were praying for.

Graham often jokes, saying that if he, who had not been a committed Christian then, had known what they were doing at the time, he probably would have fired them! Notice those elements – obedience to Jesus, love for the company and simple, yet courageous acts – were the catalysts for remarkable change in the Power Group! Through their prayer and obedience the spiritual climate of our organisation began to change. I now know that their faithful prayers were the power behind the changes that eventually took place in Graham's life and in the Power Group of companies. After all, the Bible says it so clearly: 'The prayer of a righteous man is powerful and effective' (Jas 5:16).

Do you notice that James 5:16 says that it is *righteousness*, and not your position or title, that makes your prayer effective before God? God used Eleanor's faithfulness to start a gentle revival that would not only reach many of the employees of the Power Group of companies, but it reached beyond that through Graham's life to the Global Day of Prayer, eventually touching hundreds of millions of people across the world. Of course this is how our awesome God works! God uses everybody, even the most humble person, to do his awesome work! (see 1 Corinthians 1:27)

## What does God have for You to Do?

God wants to use people, not positions, to change the world. So that means that

God wants to use you! Are you willing and available to God? If your answer is yes, then He can use you!

A friend of mine often says that 'opportunities are most often labelled as challenges'. Sometimes the challenge that you are facing in your work life, or your workplace, is just the thing that God wants to use in order to work a miracle! If God could use Joseph's obedience and courage to transform Egypt and bless Israel (see Genesis 50:20), and Eleanor's faithfulness and prayer to transform the Power Group, imagine what God could do with you. Don't let your life pass you by while you are waiting for the perfect position, or the perfect moment to serve Him! I can assure you that God has many things He wants you to do right where you are.

What Eleanor and a few colleagues started, grew from there – our company now has a number of prayer and Bible study groups that meet during the week. We are serious about bringing Jesus back to the center of the marketplace! We also have a group of twenty-four intercessors who come from outside the company to pray for the projects that we are involved in. We acknowledge the truth that 'Unless the LORD builds the house, its builders labour in vain. Unless the LORD watches over the city, the watchmen stand guard in vain' (Ps 127:1). The intercessors visit the sites on which we are building houses or roads and they pray for God's blessing on the land and the projects. They ask God to protect our employees who work there and to guard our equipment. They also ask God to bless the people who will live in the homes, or drive on the roads. Isn't that a wonderful idea!? I have heard of a company that prays over every letter and parcel they send out, asking God to bless the recipients.

These things, which we may count as insignificant, have incredible value in the spiritual realm! We may never know to what extent our little acts of obedience and faith transform the lives of others. Consider this text for just a moment, 'The weapons we fight with are not the weapons of the world. On the contrary, they have divine power to demolish strongholds' (2 Cor 10:4).

---

*These things, which we may count as insignificant, have incredible value in the spiritual realm! We may never know to what extent our little acts of obedience and faith transform the lives of others.*

---

Points to Ponder

I want to encourage you to ask God to show you how you could be used right now in your work life and workplace. Who can you start praying for today? Who else is there in your company or workplace with whom you could stand in agreement to see your bosses, or your industry, transformed? Remember that God wants to use ordinary people to do extraordinary things!

Remember that the first step in turning your ordinary day into an extraordinary calling is to live your life entirely for Jesus! You will never find blessing and joy unless you do so. What things are there in your life that you need to turn away from in order to turn to God wholeheartedly? Perhaps you have been focussing exclusively on what you want out of life. Maybe you are involved in some business dealings that are not right – anything that hinders you from living your life entirely for Jesus will draw you out of God's will and stop you from being blessed and being a blessing.

Think about the most difficult person that you encounter each day. The Bible is clear that we should love our enemies and pray for those who persecute us (see Matthew 5:44). When last did you spend a few minutes praying for that person; praying for him or her to experience blessing and peace and joy? Prayer changes people and situations! Most importantly, it can transform all those negative and destructive emotions that rob you of joy and life into emotions of blessing and thanksgiving as you witness the transforming power of love at work around you! What do you need to do in order to love the people and the place where you work more deeply? Remember, until God releases you from a position He desires you to do your best while you are there!

Acting with courage often requires support. Graham is such a wonderful example of a person who puts his love into practice! He allows God's love to lead him to reach out to people that others have turned their backs on, or to confront organisations and situations that others are afraid to engage. However, Graham never acts alone. He always seeks the support, counsel and input of others when he is going to act. The Bible is clear, 'Plans fail for lack of counsel, but with many advisers they succeed' (Prov 15:22). If you can find a few people in your workplace, or a few people from your church, who will stand with you to support, encourage and counsel you, you are far more likely to succeed in transforming your work life for Christ. Sometimes people can see opportunities that you haven't noticed, or they can simply offer you guidance about the best way to approach a difficult person or situation in a Christlike manner.

Can you see that God can use any person, in any position in a company, to bring about true transformation? I hope that you are beginning to see how God wants to use you to turn your company or workplace to Him?

Questions for Group Discussion

- Jesus said, 'With man this is impossible, but not with God; all things are possible with God' (Mark 10:27). How does this promise apply to you and your work life? What are some of the impossible things that you would like God to make possible for you?
- Why do you think God uses the 'foolish' and 'humble' things of the world to achieve great things in his kingdom?
- Can you give any examples of humble people that God has used to bring about significant changes in the world? What made it possible for them to be used by God?
- What practical things could you do in your work life in order to start influencing change and transformation?
- Eleanor's story shows that one of the best ways to transform a powerful organisation is to reach out to the people in authority and power. Who can you start praying for in your company? Commit yourself to pray for a particular group of people, the people who influence and shape your organisation, each week as a group. You will be amazed by how quickly you will see results from your prayers!
- How do you know when your work in a particular job, or company, is done? Do you think that God sometimes places us in situations that are not all that comfortable in order to develop our faith and deepen our love and character? Can you think of any instances in the Bible where people were stretched in their faith and actions so that God could use them to transform places and people? List a few of these examples and see what you can learn from each of them.
- Please pray for each member in the group. Ask God to give each of you eyes that will see the opportunities for ministry where you currently are. Pray that God will give you favour and love in order to do his will where you are, and that God will bless you with enough faith to know that He will do whatever else is necessary to bring about a Godly transformation!

People often talk about the sacred-secular divide, but my faith tells me that God is found in earth and rocks and buildings and institutions, and, yes in the business world.

– David Miller (former IBM executive)

As long as we believe that the church was born inside four walls, we will always need four walls to have church.

– Ed Silvoso

'What, after all, is Apollos? And what is Paul? Only servants, through whom you came to believe – as the Lord has assigned to each his task. I planted the seed, Apollos watered it, but God made it grow. So neither he who plants nor he who waters is anything, but only God, who makes things grow. The man who plants and the man who waters have one purpose, and each will be rewarded according to his own labour. For we are God's fellow-workers; you are God's field, God's building.'

– 1 Corinthians 3:5–9

# 11

## IDEAS FOR PASTORS, PRIESTS AND PULPIT

### Ministers: A Strategic Alliance to Transform the World!

One of the most encouraging sentences Jesus spoke must surely be, '... with God all things are possible' (Matt 19:26). Indeed, when God looks upon your town or city He can see the endless possibilities for transformation, healing, renewal and blessing! What is even more amazing is that God wants to use you and me to achieve this wonderful task – every Christian is saved to serve.

---

*... every Christian is saved to serve.*

---

In Chapter 4 we discussed the fact that God's ultimate desire is to establish his kingdom of grace, provision, blessing and wholeness on earth. Jesus came to redeem all creation by his death and resurrection (see Colossians 1:19–20), and then God poured out the Holy Spirit on believers to empower them to be his agents of blessing and transformation throughout the world. Jesus says, 'But you will receive power when the Holy Spirit comes on you; and you will be my witnesses in Jerusalem, and in all Judea and Samaria, and to the ends of the earth' (Acts 1:8).

## Pentecost: The Birth of the Church in the Pulpit and the Marketplace

When the promise of Acts 1:8 was fulfilled on Pentecost with the outpouring of the Holy Spirit on the believers, three remarkable things happened!

*Firstly*, when *God poured out the Holy Spirit* the believers received the only true source of power to transform the world by operating beyond their own abilities and gifts – the evidence of this miracle on Pentecost was the preaching of the good news in a multitude of languages (see Acts 2:6). People were amazed that ordinary Jews could speak with such skill and eloquence in a multitude of languages. This miracle resulted in the first-ever recorded revival in the marketplace! The fantastic news is that God still wants to bless believers with his supernatural power through the Holy Spirit to do things that are beyond their own abilities and gifts, in order for God's kingdom to be established for the renewal and transformation of the world.

However, on that day something broke loose, the effects of which are still being felt all across the earth by millions of people each day, more than 2 000 years later. What was that miracle which started on Pentecost that is still reaching the world? This was the second remarkable outcome of Pentecost – the miracle of *the birth of the church!* Acts 2 not only records the outpouring of God's Spirit upon believers and the fulfilment of the promise that He wants to pour out his powerful Spirit upon every believer (see the fulfilment of Joel 2:28–29 in Acts 2:17–21), but it also tells of the birth of the Christian church that started on that day. The miracle of the church has spread all across the globe in many different forms ever since – it must surely be one of the most pervasive and influential groupings of people in all human history. In Acts 2:41 we read about the baptism of the first converts (baptism still remains a sign of entry into the Christian church). Then in the verses that follow, Acts 2:42–44, we read about the different forms of ministry the early church initiated, 'They devoted themselves to the apostles' teaching and to the fellowship, to the breaking of bread and to prayer. Everyone was filled with awe, and many wonders and miraculous signs were done by the apostles. All the believers were together and had everything in common' (Acts 2:42–44). The Christian church still remains God's chosen instrument for bringing people to faith and for lovingly transforming communities through prayer, worship, teaching, ministry, miracles and caring for the needs of the community.

I have heard so many inspiring and challenging sermons that encourage believers to pray to be filled with God's Holy Spirit in order to operate in God's transforming power. I have also seen many incredible models of church and Christian community that have been used by God to proclaim the Gospel and bring tangible and real transformation across the world.

However, a *third* critical thing happened on that Pentecost day that I have seldom heard churches and pastors preach about; on Pentecost a *strategic ministry alliance* between pulpit ministry and marketplace ministry was initiated. Acts 2 has two major scenes:

The first scene is the outpouring of the Holy Spirit. As the believers are baptised with the Holy Spirit they immediately fulfil the promise of Acts 1:8 and become witnesses in Jerusalem, and because of the gift of preaching in different languages their influence spreads in the weeks that follow into Judea, Samaria and to the ends of the known world. All those who heard the Gospel in their own languages in the marketplace came to know Christ (see Acts 2:6–12) and they took the message with them into the world (Acts 2:41). The first move of God's Spirit was through the believers into the marketplace.

The second major scene in Acts 2 is a modelling of pulpit ministry. As the Spirit of God enables Peter, he stands up and preaches a message of repentance (see Acts 2:14–40). God uses his message to touch the hearts of those who are gathered and about 3000 people come to know Christ as their Savior on that day (see Acts 2:41)! Then the apostles formed a community of worship, teaching, prayer and care – the birth of the first congregation!

## The Church and the Congregations

If one studies Acts 2 in this manner you will see that the church is much broader than the congregations. The establishment of the church comes first as people are brought into a living relationship with God in Christ, and then the work of the congregation is birthed to support, encourage, enliven, empower and fuel the lives of the believers. Understanding this relationship is critical if we are going to overcome some of the false understandings that have crippled and undermined ministry in the WHOLE church, through the pulpit and the marketplace. God has one church, but there are varying tasks, a variety of expressions, multiple locations and some specialisations that need to have space and encouragement to develop in order for God's kingdom to be established everywhere.

> *God has one church, but there are varying tasks, a variety of expressions, multiple locations and some specialisations that need to have space and encouragement to develop in order for God's kingdom to be established everywhere.*

Paul expresses this very sentiment when he writes to the Corinthian believers, saying: 'What, after all, is Apollos? And what is Paul? Only servants, through whom you came to believe – as the Lord has assigned to each his task. I planted the seed, Apollos watered it, but God made it grow. So neither he who plants nor he who waters is anything, but only God, who makes things grow. The man who plants and the man who waters have one purpose, and each will be rewarded according to his own labour. For we are God's fellow-workers; you are God's field,

God's building' (1 Corinthians 3:5–9).

What we need is to form a strategic and powerful alliance between what gifted, skilled and committed people are doing in pulpit ministries (by this I mean congregations with Sunday services, groups, outreach ministries and so forth) and people who are engaged in marketplace ministries (by this I mean kingdom-minded business people who are evangelising in their sphere of influence, working hard to transform both people and systems for the kingdom of God).

## Mindshifts for a Powerful Ministry Alliance!

I had to go through a major paradigm shift in order to realise that this partnership of pulpit and marketplace ministries was God's will for 'my church'. In my mind I knew that the church was not the building in which we met on a Sunday, nor was it the sum of the activities that were arranged, supported and facilitated by my local congregation – I understood, in my mind at least, that the church is the 'body of Christ' which gathers at certain times for necessary and specific tasks (such as worship, fellowship, teaching and so forth) and scatters into the world for other tasks (such as ministry, evangelism, mission and transformation). However, the reality was that as a pastor, the majority of my time, energy and creativity was focussed on the life and activities around the church building!

*The reality is that most pastors focus the majority of their time, energy and creativity on the life and activities that happen in and around their church building!*

When Graham came to Christ, I was suddenly challenged by an entirely different perspective on ministry and community transformation. Here is a guy who loves the Lord passionately. Not only that, but he is also serious about using all of his life, not just the time spent on church activities, to honour God. For the first time I realised that this is what God wants for every member of my congregation – God doesn't just want a part of our lives, or some of our time, God wants everything! Graham knew that and he was eager to be obedient to God's calling.

As a pastor I was challenged to consider the question – in what way does God want to use the members of this congregation in ministry? For most of my time in ministry I believed that the best way for someone to serve the Lord was in some form of ministry or service in the congregation. So, if you are a teacher and you love Jesus you should be teaching others in the church, using your gift to share the truth of the Gospel. If you are blessed with the gift of 'getting things done', then my aim would be to get you into one of our mission projects. There you could use your gift to help the ministry become effective, streamlined and focussed. However, as is the case with most pastors, it seldom crossed my mind that the reason why my members had particular gifts was not to support the work of the church, but rather to use these gifts in order to transform the world!

Shortly after Graham's conversion we watched George Otis' video *Transformations*. I was deeply moved by a sentence that one of the people in the documentary said. This pastor said, 'One day when I give an account to God of my ministry, God is not going to ask me how I pastored my congregation, but how I pastored my city.'

> *When you give an account of your ministry, God is not going to ask how you pastored your congregation, but how you pastored your city.*

I soon came to realise that my responsibility was to pastor my congregation in such a way that we could truly begin to transform our city. Building a big church would be less important to God than truly transforming the community in which our church was built.

In order to do this I would have to change the focus of my ministry. Instead of focussing on equipping the members to serve only in the church, I had to spend time and energy finding out what their needs are from Monday to Friday, from eight in the morning till five in the afternoon. If you are a pastor reading this chapter, tell me, when last did you visit your members in their workplace? It is not possible to hear God's will for your members effectively unless you know where they are, what they are doing and what they are struggling with. You cannot preach and teach with real effectiveness unless you are allowing God to take you to the places where you can see what He wants to do with 'your' congregation.

Sadly, as I have spoken to many of my colleagues in pastoral ministry, most of them have indicated that they have only ever visited their members at work when they have needed something (like help with a broken motor car, or money for a project the church is undertaking). Conversely, when I have spoken to

Christians who are ministering and serving Christ in the marketplace, they have expressed frustration and disappointment at the lack of support they get from their pastors. Many of them fear that their pastor only sees them as a source of funds.

Pastors, visiting your members in their workplace is the 'home visit' of our age! They spend most of their time and energy at work. How wonderful it would be if you could offer to pop in and see them where they work. We invite the pastors of our staff at the Power Group to visit their members in our offices. Sometimes they will just pop in to say 'Hi'! At other times they will come in to share a message with a larger group. Sometimes they will stop by their member's office to pray for the work they are doing. This creates such a strong connection between the member and his or her pastor!

Just as a pastor has a unique calling and therefore unique gifts to bless people with, marketplace ministers often also have a particular calling, matched with particular gifts, with which to bless the body of Christ. Our cities would be truly blessed if the whole church (pulpit and marketplace) could learn to use their respective focuses and gifts in order to achieve God's will for the whole city – not just the congregation. As a pulpit minister I have found that my years of study and work in the congregation have developed pastoral skills, Biblical insight, a calling to prayer, and strong focus on relationships. I can use these to support people, offer them courage and hope, help them to listen for God's voice and figure out how to deal with particular problems from a Biblical perspective. Graham, on the other hand, has honed his ability to think big, to take risks, to push through obstacles and to work for the achievement of goals. As Graham and I have worked together we have been blessed by each other's gifts and abilities, inside and outside the congregation.

We are one church, a church that gathers for certain events and a church that scatters for others. By cultivating the clear understanding that the ministry of the church stretches beyond the congregation you can be a church that meets throughout the week, ministering in a multitude of settings and expressions, yet working toward a single purpose – establishing God's kingdom in your city.

## From a Suburb to the World!

One of the common fears that I have heard from pastors and ministers is the fear that their marketplace members will 'take over' the church. There is little doubt that some congregations do suffer under the demands and expectations of members who control the church through their influence or giving. However, my experience has been that if you cultivate a number of strong, committed, courageous, Christlike marketplace leaders in your congregation they will have the authority and ability to hold one another accountable and engage one another on an equal footing.

That being said, there is so much more to be gained by supporting, encouraging and celebrating the work that God wants to do through the marketplace ministers in your congregation! As I explained in Chapter 1, I was extremely tempted to 'hijack' all Graham's gifting for exclusive use in the ministry of my congregation. I thank God that He prevented that!

God spoke very clearly to Graham and has given him two clear instructions. The first came when God told Graham to hire the Newlands Rugby Stadium in Cape Town and to call all the Christians together for a day of repentance and prayer. He did it – and so the Global Day of Prayer was born. In 2001 an amazing number of 48 000 Christians gathered at the stadium for worship and prayer. It took the big thinking, fearlessness and straightforward obedience of a business-man to make it happen! While the churches were arguing about whether they would support the event, asking what denomination Graham came from, finding out which bishops, pastors and ministers would be participating, Graham was mobilising thousands of people for prayer. God honoured that, and today the Global Day of Prayer operates in every country in the world with more than 350 million believers gathering in homes, stadiums and churches on Pentecost Sunday. Please visit http://www.globaldayofprayer.com for more information.

Then, in 2006 God gave Graham a second clear instruction, the challenge that Christians should make a stand for values, ethics and clean living. Since then we have been travelling all over the world with remarkable results as people have com-mitted themselves to 'turn from their wicked ways' (2 Chron 7:14). Please see http://www.unashamedlyethical.com and Chapter 12 for more on this wonderful initiative.

I could never have achieved this, and if I had limited Graham's influence to my congregation only, a small Methodist Church in Cape Town, this wonderful move of God may never have taken place. The truth is that God wants to use every Christian to do extraordinary things, but they need support, equipping and care to discover and develop their gifts and talents for God's kingdom.

I am certain that there are hundreds of Graham Powers in your city! God is wait-ing for the right moment to release something spectacular, something unique, through their life and ministry. Perhaps your congregation could be the launching pad that gives them just that little bit of encouragement and support that sets them on their way?

# Some Practical Pointers for Pastors

Points to Ponder

There are so many things that you can do in order to support and develop the ministry of your members for a marketplace ministry. The first step is surely to commit yourself before God to raise them up for the work that God has called them to! Why not call a few of the marketplace ministers in your congregation and set up an appointment to see them at work. Go there to bless them, pray for them and ask them to help you to birth a marketplace ministry from your congregation. In our congregation we started with a 'cell group' to which Graham and Lauren and a few other marketplace friends were invited.

Next, I would encourage you to study some of the excellent resources on marketplace ministry. Ed Silvoso and Os Hillman's books in particular have been a great help. There are many other wonderful resources that will help you in this task.

I would like to encourage you to consider a few basic 'first steps' in establishing a strategic partnership in ministry with your various marketplace members.

- *Pray for your marketplace ministers*. Get the names and business names of the marketplace ministers in your congregation and begin to pray for them and their businesses. God has something special for each of them to do. Ask God to protect and help them in their work, and to create a hunger to move from a success paradigm to a significance and obedience paradigm in their work life. Pray for their employees and their families and ask God to deepen their relationship with Him.
- *Develop your marketplace ministers*. Graham had to learn many things about his potential, God's calling and his responsibility as a marketplace minister in those early years. I know of very few churches that do intentional work to develop and support their marketplace ministers for ministry in the marketplace. This is not as daunting a task as it may seem. Simply start by helping your members to discover their gifts. Next, help them to connect their gifts and abilities to what they are already doing or facing each day. Pray with them, listen with them and help them to discern God's call for their lives. Then find ways to equip them with the knowledge and skills they will need to fulfil God's calling in their workplace.
- *Visit your marketplace ministers at work*. Make the time to visit your marketplace

ministers on 'their turf'. Go there with one simple intention – to bless them. Try to sustain this pastoral discipline in the midst of the demands of your ministry. You will not be sorry! As you visit, ask God to show you things about the people, the systems and the place. This will enable you to pray 'on site with insight'.

- *Create opportunities for building relationships and co-operation between your marketplace ministers.* Business is central to business people! If you can connect a few marketplace ministers around business opportunities and tasks, the benefits will win great favour. It is important to trust the people that you connect with one another. Another benefit of building relationships between marketplace believers is that they will mentor and disciple one another. I know very little about business, but when Graham was saved he could connect with some key business leaders who were more mature in their faith and who could offer him clear and practical Christian advice and help.

- *Recognise and celebrate God's work in the marketplace.* I started a slot called 'Acts 29' in one of my churches. This was an opportunity for us to share testimonies of what God is doing through the marketplace ministers in our congregation. Not only did these testimonies enliven the faith life of our congregation, connecting us with many different and wonderful projects throughout the city, they also offered an opportunity for the congregation to celebrate and acknowledge the ministry of our marketplace ministers! In fact, I would go so far as to suggest that you should regularly commission marketplace ministers in your church services. Have a service in which you celebrate the ministry that members are doing in the community. We would often do this with teachers, doctors and safety and security personnel. Invite these members to a special event where you help them to catch the vision of using their work as ministry. Then have a public service of worship during which you commission them from your congregation as your missionaries and ministers in the marketplace!

- *Bless your marketplace ministers.* Finally, I would encourage you to get your congregation behind the ministries of the marketplace ministers. Most often the flow is in the opposite direction – from the marketplace into the congregation. Why not bless your marketplace ministers by finding ways to support what they are doing? For example, our church supplies people, food and blankets to a homeless ministry that was started from a business run by one of our members. Or, as I have already mentioned, the pastors of our employees often visit the Power Group to pray with us, encourage us and express their appreciation and care.

Remember that the best blessings are most often practical and they address a clearly felt need.

I am sure that you will be able to find, and share, many more creative and practical suggestions for supporting and equipping your members for marketplace ministry. We simply need to remember that God has called us to the same task. We all have different abilities and gifts, but one ultimate purpose, namely to establish God's kingdom on earth.

Make the commitment to shift from being a pastor to your church only, to being a pastor to your community as well. You won't be sorry!

Questions for Group Discussion
- Why did God create the Christian church?
- What specific role and function should a pastor or minister fulfil in the community?
- How could you encourage and support your pastor to be more supportive of marketplace ministers?
- Please take some time to thank God for the life of your church's pastor. Pray that God will give your pastor a heart for the city and that God will reveal the importance and the principles of ministry in the marketplace to him or her.
- I would encourage your group to pray regularly for your pastor. Moreover, since the biggest changes come through love, I would encourage you to find a tangible way to care for your pastor, while at the same time asking God to give you an opportunity to enrich his or her ministry by introducing them to the principles of marketplace ministry.

Let your holy life, your pure conversation, and your faithful
instruction, be everywhere seen and known. Always, in all societies, in all business, at home
and abroad, in prosperity and adversity, let it be seen that you are real Christians.
– Bible commentator Albert Barnes (1798 – 1870)
commenting on Matthew 5:16


'You are the light of the world. A city that is set on a hill cannot be hidden. Nor do they
light a lamp and put it under a basket, but on a lampstand, and it gives light to all who are in the
house. Let your light so shine before men, that they may see your good works
and glorify your Father in heaven.'
– Matthew 5:14–16 (NKJV)

# 12

## VALUES, ETHICS AND CLEAN LIVING

### Unashamedly Ethical and the Global Day of Prayer
#### – WRITTEN BY STEVEN JOHNSTONE

Since the day that I was born again, I have always loved seeing and hearing of people who have come to faith in Christ, and I love to hear of their lives and conduct being transformed. And why not? After all, it is God Himself who 'desires all men to be saved' (1 Tim 2:3–4, NKJV) and so if we have been born of God's Spirit we will also desire the salvation of the world.

Graham Power is an example of such a story. When he committed his life to Christ it was for him, as he puts it, a '24/7-commitment'. And this showed in his personal and professional life. Indeed, the Power Group of companies itself went through a rigorous overhaul to ensure that its policies and practices were in line with God's Word – something for which Graham took much criticism and something for which I deeply respect him.

Stories like the transformation of Graham and his companies inspire us. As Christians we love to talk about and pray for revival. We love reading the old revival stories and we long to see God do it again in our generation. And rightly so. But what is our responsibility to God, and to the world, to see revival happen?

*What is our responsibility to God, and to the world, to see revival happen?*

Before we get ahead of ourselves, first a little background on the Unashamedly Ethical campaign that I co-ordinate. Unashamedly Ethical is a campaign working closely with the Global Day of Prayer, and together we seek to bring God's transforming power to the world.

As with the Global Day of Prayer, Unashamedly Ethical was birthed by Graham Power. And just as the Global Day was designed to challenge Christians to 'humble themselves, pray and seek my [God's] face' (2 Chron 7:14a), the Unashamedly Ethical campaign is designed to challenge people to 'turn from their wicked ways' (2 Chron 7:14b).

We trust that the campaign, started in October 2006, will be instrumental in causing a wave of good values, ethics and clean living to sweep the globe.

The campaign is built upon three pillars, around which local communities are formed:

- Firstly, the campaign challenges all people to make a public commitment to good values, ethics and clean living. These commitments are made by signing the relevant Unashamedly Ethical commitment forms (see Appendix).
- Secondly, we have established an online directory of all our signatories (individual and organizational signatories) which can be searched at www.unashamedlyethical.com. In this way, we have made it easy for our signatories to find and trade with each other.
- And thirdly, we have a presiding ombudsman who holds all our signatories accountable. The ombudsman will receive and investigate any complaint against a signatory.

Our strategy is to form local communities of signatories all over the world. Each local Unashamedly Ethical community is run by its own committee, meets regularly, and relationships form within the community around this inherently Biblical topic. Our strategy is then designed to take advantage of the discipleship and evangelistic opportunities which these relationships lead to.

Please visit our website (www.unashamedlyethical.com) to learn more about how we can help you use the campaign as a powerful tool to disciple other believers, and a stunningly effective evangelistic tool to reach unbelievers, all right in the heart of the marketplace!

## Revival and Responsibility

I am persuaded that there are two overwhelming responsibilities that we as Christians have if we are serious about seeing God's power transform our world. Firstly, we have a responsibility to live holy lives ourselves, marked by good values, ethics and clean living. Secondly, we have a responsibility to take the message of the Gospel into the world.

# Our Responsibility to Good Values, Ethics and Clean Living

*'For the grace of God that brings salvation has appeared to all men. It teaches us to say "No" to ungodliness and worldly passions, and to live self-controlled, upright and godly lives in this present age, while we wait for the blessed hope – the glorious appearing of our great God and Savior, Jesus Christ, who gave himself for us to redeem us from all wickedness and to purify for himself a people that are his very own, eager to do what is good. These, then, are the things you should teach. Encourage and rebuke with all authority. Do not let anyone despise you.'*

– TITUS 2:11–15

It is surprising to me how many Christians struggle with the concept of a campaign promoting good values, ethics and clean living – as if it were a 'gospel of works'. Paul told Timothy that 'these, then, are the things you *should* teach.' To me it is a joy to be associated with a growing community of people all around the world who are committing themselves publicly to saying '"No" to ungodliness and worldly passions' and to living 'self-controlled, upright and godly lives in this present age'.

Of course, God desires us to live Godly lives simply because it is right and pleasing to Him. But what fascinates me is that the Bible clearly teaches that there is another reason why God demands Godly living from us.

## The Witness of a Clean Life

Paul told Philemon that the sharing of his faith would become effective when people acknowledged every good thing in Christ (see Philemon 1:4–6).

I have lost count of the vast number of business people who have told me that some of their worst experiences in business have been with 'so-called Christians'.

How have we slipped so far that the major indicators of immorality are no different in the church than in the world? Abortion, divorce, pre-marital sex, tax evasion, drunkenness and a host of other ungodly acts appear as consistently amongst Christians as they do amongst unbelievers. It is a scandal in Heaven!

And all the while, the world is watching.

Jesus said that we are the light of the world and the salt of the earth. But He also warned that if salt loses its saltiness it will be regarded as worthless and trampled by men. Isn't this a sad description of the witness of so many Christian people?

If you are a Christian, you are an ambassador of Christ. You no longer live for yourself, but you are to live for Him who died for you. Everything you do, and every word you say, is a reflection of Christ to the world. And the world will think more, or less, of the Gospel depending on the conduct of those of us who claim to have been transformed by it.

---

*The world will think more, or less, of the Gospel depending on the conduct of those of us who claim to have been transformed by it.*

---

Yes, there is grace for the Christian, but if we read the verses I quoted from Titus 2 again, we are reminded that if we have truly come to know God's grace, it then teaches us 'to live self-controlled, upright and godly lives in this present age'.

Paul told Titus, 'Teach slaves to be subject to their masters in everything, to try to please them, not to talk back to them, and not to steal from them, but to show that they can be fully trusted, so that in every way they will make the teaching about God our Savior attractive' (Tit 2:9–10).

What a wonderful way of putting it! When we live ethical, peaceful lives, we make the message of our Savior attractive to the world.

Peter pleads with us in 1 Pet 2:11–12 (NKJV), 'Beloved, I beg you as sojourners and pilgrims, abstain from fleshly lusts which war against the soul, having your conduct honourable among the Gentiles, that when they speak against you as evildoers, they may, by your good works which they observe, glorify God in the day of visitation.'

And so if we want revival and transformation to come to our countries, if we want 'the day of visitation' to arrive, part of our responsibility is to shine our light to the world through lives marked by good values, ethics and clean living. Make your own public commitment to this today by visiting http://www.unashamedly-ethical.com and completing the relevant commitment form.

In our pursuit of revival and transformation, there is another responsibility that falls squarely upon our shoulders.

## Our Responsibility to Take the Gospel into All the World

Prayer is often touted as the only 'key to revival'. I deeply appreciate the importance of prayer in every facet of the Christian life. However, we need to be careful that we do not exalt prayer to the exclusion of our evangelistic responsibilities. I have encountered some believers who neglect their responsibility to proclaim the Word of God, choosing only to intercede for the lost from the safety of their churches, commanding strongholds to fall, and binding satanic forces. In prayer we call the unbelieving world into the kingdom, and we beg God to come and save all people. We remind ourselves that the 'effective, fervent prayer of a righteous man avails much' (Jas 5:16, NKJV), and so we pray for the lost, and then we wait. And we wait. And we pray some more. And then we wait more, as if God's plan to reveal the Gospel to the world does not involve our fervent action in conjunction with our ardent prayer.

Paul said, 'How then shall they call on Him in whom they have not believed? And how shall they believe in Him of whom they have not heard? And how shall they hear without a preacher? And how shall they preach unless they are sent. As it is written, "How beautiful are the feet of those who preach the gospel of peace, who bring glad tidings of good things!"' (Rom 10:14–15, NKJV)

For a long time I have had a conviction and a passion to spur believers on to take up the critically important task of preaching to the lost. Prayer is not a replacement for sharing the Gospel with the lost. Indeed, we do read in 1 Timothy 2:1–7 and Romans 10:1 that we are to pray for the lost. However, it is important to understand that in both cases Paul also strongly makes the case that it is preachers, and the preaching of the Gospel, that will achieve that which is being prayed for.

On the other hand though, there are countless exhortations for Christians to pray for preachers, and for the preaching of the Gospel to spread. Read these four Scriptures as a start: Luke 10:2, Ephesians 6:18–20, Colossians 4:2–4 and 2 Thessalonians 3:1, and in each case ask yourself, 'Who and what are we being told to pray for?'

Jesus did not say, 'Stay in your corner and call all the world to come to you.' No, He said 'Go into all the world and preach the gospel!' (Mark 16:15, NKJV). If we want revival, prayer is essential, but so is the preaching of the Gospel! We must by all means and in every way possible find ways to get the truth of God's Word to the unbelieving world around us. And if this is going to happen then we must under-stand that it has little to do with church buildings. It requires creative, committed Christians finding ways to reach their own communities with God's Word.

Jesus said, 'The harvest is plentiful, but the workers are few. Ask the Lord of the harvest, therefore, to send out workers into his harvest field' (Luke 10:2).

According to Jesus, the problem is not that there is insufficient interest in God on the part of unbelievers. The problem is rather that there are not enough people willing to be labourers. And I strongly believe that one of the reasons for this is that most Christians don't know how to reach their communities with God's Word, and so they don't! But I am equally convinced that with a bit of thought, creativity and collaboration, every one of us can find resourceful ways to reach more of the lost with the Gospel.

# Taking Responsibility

The Unashamedly Ethical campaign is taking responsibility in both of the areas I have discussed. Firstly, we aim to challenge believers to be the salt and light God has called us to be in the world, and we facilitate the forming of local communities to provide focussed discussion and ongoing encouragement, specifically around clean and ethical living. Secondly, the campaign is also designed to help all Christians create a platform for building marketplace-based relationships with unbelievers that can lead to their salvation and their being established in God's Word.

Visit www.unashamedlyethical.com to learn about starting your own local Unashamedly Ethical community.

Points to Ponder and Questions for Group Discussion
As Christians who want to live clean and ethical lives, it may be helpful to many of us to pray about the following:

- To Ponder: 'All Scripture is given by inspiration of God, and is profitable for doctrine, for reproof, for correction, for instruction in righteousness, that the man of God may be complete, thoroughly equipped for every good work.' (2 Tim 3:16–17, NKJV)

- God's most powerful tool for the transformation of a person is his Word, the Bible. But a study has shown that ninety-eight percent of professing born-again Christians have never taken the time to read the Bible from Genesis to Revelation – not even once! Let me encourage you to commit your life to reading the totality of God's Word at least annually, and watch how He will work in your life.

- Questions for Group Discussion: Have you ever read the Bible from cover to cover? Do you read God's Word on a daily basis? Do you have a systematic plan of Bible reading? If this is a weakness in your faith life, what practical changes need to take place in your life for you to correct it?

- To Ponder: 'Let us hold fast the confession of our hope without wavering, for He who promised is faithful. And let us consider one another in order to stir up love and good works, not forsaking the assembling of ourselves together, as is the manner of some, but exhorting one another, and so much the more as you see the Day approaching' (Heb 10:23–25, NKJV).

- God uses people. When we surround ourselves with Godly people, we can be encouraged to hold onto our faith, and be stirred up to love and good works. But how many of us can truly say that we are in close fellowship with other believers and regularly have deliberate, transparent discussions about our own lives regarding clean and ethical living?

- Questions for Group Discussion: Make a list of the ten people you spend most of your time with. Now ask yourself, do these people build you up or tear you down? What can you do to spend more time with good people to whom you can speak openly, and by whom you can be challenged, be held accountable and be encouraged?

- To Ponder: Jesus said, 'The harvest is plentiful, but the workers are few. Ask the Lord of the harvest, therefore, to send out workers into his harvest field' (Luke 10:2). I believe that if most Christian business people put as much creative thought and entrepreneurial flair into reaching the marketplace with God's Word as they do into building their businesses, we would be in the middle of a huge revival.

- Questions for Group Discussion: If you were guaranteed to receive $10 million in cash in twelve months' time provided you could, sometime within that period, successfully run a sixteen-week evangelistic Bible study with twenty unsaved colleagues/friends, what would you do to get the job done?

*Steve Johnstone is the International Co-ordinator of Unashamedly Ethical, a movement challenging people to clean and ethical living, and helping all Christians take the Gospel to their communities.*

*Visit http://www.unashamedlyethical.com*

# FURTHER READING AND VIEWING:

- Buford, Bob. *Halftime: Changing Your Game Plan from Success to Significance.* Zondervan, 1994.
- Hillman, Os. *Faith@Work.* Aslan Publishing, 2004.
- Hillman, Os. *The 9 to 5 Window.* Regal Books, 2005.
- Johnson, Brett. *Convergence: Integrating Your Career, Community, Creativity and Calling.* Indaba Publishing, 2009.
- Joubert, Willem. *Luke 10 Transformation.* The Better Way Foundation Trust, 2007.
- Otis Jr, George. *Transformations.* (DVD)
- Power, Graham and Vermooten, Diane. *Not by Might Nor by Power.* Creation House Publishers, 2009.
- Reeb, Lloyd. *From Success to Significance: When the Pursuit of Success Isn't Enough.* Zondervan, 2004.
- Reeb, Lloyd and Wellons, Bill. *Unlimited Partnership: Igniting a Marketplace Leader's Journey to Eternal Significance.* B&H Books, 2007.
- Silvoso, Ed. *That None Should Perish: How to Reach Entire Cities for Christ through Prayer Evangelism.* Regal Books, 1994.
- Silvoso, Ed. *Prayer Evangelism.* Regal Books, 2000.
- Silvoso, Ed. *Transformation: Change the Marketplace and You Change the World.* Regal Books, 2007.
- Silvoso, Ed. *Anointed for Business.* 2nd edition, Regal Books, 2009.
- Wallace, William. *Braveheart* (movie, 1995). http://www.imdb.com/title/tt0112573/quotes. Accessed 7 December 2009, 13h35

# SPORTSPERSON'S
# COMMITMENT FORM

**UNASHAMEDLY**ETHICAL

I commit:

01. Always to sing our national anthem with pride.
02. To not use illegal performance enhancing substances.
03. To treat other athletes with respect and dignity.
04. Never to accept or solicit any bribes and to report those who do.
05. To be a good role model, on and off the field.
06. To practice and compete wholeheartedly.
07. To compete within the rules.
08. To show respect for referees, umpires and other officials, and accept their decisions.
09. To pursue victory within the constraints of good sportsmanship.
10. To be gracious in victory and accept defeat with dignity, and show sincere respect in pre- and post-game rituals.

Signature _____

Signed on the _____ day of _____ , 20 _____ in _____

By signing this form I agree that my information may be added to the Unashamedly Ethical database for the use of future communication. I also agree that if I do not abide within the Ombudsman's Code of Conduct (available at www.unashamedlyethical.com) I will be held accountable for such conduct by the Ombudsman.

Please complete the following:

Name and Surname: _____

Name of Organisation / Team / Sport: _____

E-mail Address: _____

Telephone Number: _____ Mobile Number: _____

Your Postal Address: _____

_____

_____

Please fax or e-mail the completed form to the Office:
Tel: +27 (0) 21 702 4882   Fax: +27 86 673 9720
E-mail: info@unashamedlyethical.com
Web: www.unashamedlyethical.com
PO Box 3856 Somerset West 7129

# YOUTH INDIVIDUAL
## COMMITMENT FORM

**UNASHAMEDLY**ETHICAL

I commit:

01. To tell the truth always.
02. To honour my parents, and to respect my teachers.
03. To stay pure in all my relationships.
04. To do what is right even when my friends do not do so.
05. To be unselfish, and to treat people like I want to be treated.
06. To stay free from alcohol and drugs.
07. To refuse to cheat on any exams or tests.
08. To do my work wholeheartedly.
09. To serve the poor in my community.
10. To collaborate with my peers to impact our community and nation.

Signature

Signed on the _____ day of _____ , 20 ____ in _____

By signing this form I agree that my information may be added to the Unashamedly Ethical database for the use of future communication. I also agree that if I do not abide within the Ombudsman's Code of Conduct (available at www.unashamedlyethical.com) I will be held accountable for such conduct by the Ombudsman.

Please complete the following:

Name and Surname: _____

Name of School/College: _____

E-mail Address: _____ Web Address: _____

Telephone Number: _____ Mobile Number: _____

Your Postal Address: _____

_____

_____

Please fax or e-mail the completed form to the Office:
Tel: +27 (0) 21 702 4882  Fax: +27 86 673 9720
E-mail: info@unashamedlyethical.com
Web: www.unashamedlyethical.com
PO Box 3856 Somerset West 7129

# INDIVIDUAL
## COMMITMENT FORM

**UNASHAMEDLY**ETHICAL

**I commit:**

01. To be entirely truthful in all I say.
02. To be faithful to my family relationships.
03. To do nothing out of selfish ambition or conceit, but to look out for the interests of others.
04. To refuse to elicit, accept or pay any bribes, and to report those who do.
05. To be a diligent leader without being harsh, and to pay my staff what is just and fair.
06. To be a peacemaker.
07. To do my work wholeheartedly.
08. To submit myself to just and ethical governing authorities.
09. To remember the poor by investing generously and sacrificially in the broader community.
10. To collaborate with my peers to impact our community and nation.

Signature _____

Signed on the _____ day of _____ , 20 _____ in _____

By signing this form I agree that my information may be added to the Unashamedly Ethical database for the use of future communication. I also agree that if I do not abide within the Ombudsman's Code of Conduct (available at www.unashamedlyethical.com) I will be held accountable for such conduct by the Ombudsman.

**Please complete the following:**

Name and Surname: _____

Name of Organization: _____

E-mail Address: _____ Web Address: _____

Telephone Number: _____ Mobile Number: _____

Your Postal Address: _____

_____

_____

Please fax or e-mail the completed form to the Office:
Tel: +27 (0) 21 702 4882  Fax: +27 86 673 9720
E-mail: info@unashamedlyethical.com
Web: www.unashamedlyethical.com
PO Box 3856 Somerset West 7129

# BUSINESS ORGANIZATIONAL
## COMMITMENT FORM

**UNASHAMEDLY**ETHICAL

As a business organization we are committed to being **UNASHAMEDLY**ETHICAL.
Accordingly, we commit:

01. To be honest and ethical in all our dealings.
02. To provide efficient, economic and effective products and services in an impartial manner.
03. To provide all stakeholders with timely, accessible and accurate information.
04. To refuse to elicit, accept or pay any bribes, and to report those who do.
05. To negotiate all contracts with the utmost integrity.
06. To pay taxes, and to pay all creditors on time.
07. To pay reasonable salaries and wages.
08. To submit ourselves to just and ethical governing authorities.
09. To remember the poor by investing generously and sacrificially in the broader community.
10. To collaborate with our peers to impact our community and nation.

Signature _____ , as authorised to sign on behalf

of _____

(name of organization)

Signed on the _____ day of _____ , 20 _____ in _____

By signing this form I agree that our information may be added to the Unashamedly Ethical database
for the use of future communication, and that our organization will be listed on the Online Directory.
I also agree that if we do not abide within the Ombudsman's Code of Conduct (available at
www.unashamedlyethical.com) we will be held accountable for such conduct by the Ombudsman.

Please complete the following:

Name and Surname of contact person: _____

Name of Organization: _____

Industry: _____

E-mail Address: _____ Web Address: _____

Telephone Number: _____ Mobile Number: _____

Your Postal Address: _____

Please fax or e-mail the completed form to the Office:
Tel: +27 (0) 21 702 4882  Fax: +27 86 673 9720
E-mail: info@unashamedlyethical.com
Web: www.unashamedlyethical.com
PO Box 3856 Somerset West 7129

155

# CHURCH ORGANIZATIONAL
## COMMITMENT FORM

**UNASHAMEDLY**ETHICAL

As a church organization we are committed to being **UNASHAMEDLY**ETHICAL.
Accordingly, we commit:

01. To be honest and ethical in all our dealings.
02. To seek the maturity of our members by encouraging them to read the whole Bible regularly.
03. To equip our members to transform every sphere of society.
04. To work towards unity within the Body of Christ.
05. To collaborate with our peers to impact our community and nation.
06. To commit a growing percentage of our resources to evangelism, Kingdom expansion and transformation by investing beyond our local ministry.
07. To care for the poor and for widows, orphans and strangers.
08. To spend the tithes and offerings we receive ethically and prayerfully.
09. To pay reasonable salaries and wages to our staff.
10. To manifest the Kingdom of God tangibly.

Signature _____ , as authorised to sign on behalf

of _____ (name of organization)

Signed on the _____ day of _____ , 20 _____ in _____

By signing this form we agree that our information may be added to the Unashamedly Ethical database for the use of future communication, and that our organization will be listed on the Online Directory. We also agree that if we do not abide within the Ombudsman's Code of Conduct (available at www.unashamedlyethical.com) we will be held accountable for such conduct by the Ombudsman.

Please complete the following:

Name and Surname of contact person: _____

Name of Organization: _____

E-mail Address: _____ Web Address: _____

Telephone Number: _____ Mobile Number: _____

Your Postal Address: _____

_____

Nature of your Ministry: _____

**Please fax or e-mail the completed form to the Office:**
Tel: +27 (0) 21 702 4882  Fax: +27 86 673 9720
E-mail: info@unashamedlyethical.com
Web: www.unashamedlyethical.com
PO Box 3856 Somerset West 7129

# GOVERNMENT/POLITICAL ORGANIZATIONAL
## COMMITMENT FORM

**UNASHAMEDLY**ETHICAL

As a government or political organization we are committed to being **UNASHAMEDLY**ETHICAL.
Accordingly, we commit:

01. To be honest and ethical in all our dealings.
02. To provide efficient, economic and effective public service delivery in an impartial and fair manner.
03. To refuse to elicit, accept or pay any bribes, and to report those who do.
04. To expect our members to disclose all personal or family financial interests which may affect their decision making.
05. To negotiate all government contracts with the utmost integrity.
06. To report fraud, corruption, nepotism, maladministration and other offenses.
07. To ensure transparency, accountability and fair administrative action by providing the public with timely, accessible and accurate information.
08. To invest in the betterment of our employees and elected officials by good human resource management.
09. To pursue the transformation of our sphere of influence and expertise in the public service.
10. To collaborate with our peers to impact the world positively.

Signature _____ , as authorised to sign on behalf

of _____ (name of organization)

Signed on the _____ day of _____ , 20 _____ in _____

By signing this form we agree that our information may be added to the Unashamedly Ethical database for the use of future communication, and that our organization will be listed on the Online Directory. We also agree that if we do not abide within the Ombudsman's Code of Conduct (available at www.unashamedlyethical.com) we will be held accountable for such conduct by the Ombudsman.

Please complete the following:

Name and Surname of contact person: _____

Name of Organization: _____

E-mail Address: _____ Web Address: _____

Telephone Number: _____ Mobile Number: _____

Your Postal Address: _____

Nature of your Organization or Department: _____

Please fax or e-mail the completed form to the Office:
Tel: +27 (0) 21 702 4882  Fax: +27 86 673 9720
E-mail: info@unashamedlyethical.com
Web: www.unashamedlyethical.com
PO Box 3856 Somerset West 7129

# BRING MEANING TO YOUR WORK

HOW GREAT LEADERS LIVE THEIR
FAITH IN THE GLOBAL MARKETPLACE

OUR
SOULS
AT
WORK

edited by
MARK L RUSSELL

foreword by DAVE GIBBONS

37 marketplace leaders, including CEO's and executives from global companies and emerging social entrepreneurs, write about putting their faith to work in the global marketplace.

*Our Souls at Work gives thought-provoking, conversation-creating, faith-growing insights based on timeless wisdom and practical experience.*

LEARN FROM GLOBAL LEADERS AND WHY THEY SAY:

"How do we fulfill the [work] calling we have been given and still be good husbands and wives and parents? It's the biggest challenge out there."

**Steve Reinemund - former CEO and Chairman of PepsiCo**

"It is not optional to give people freedom to make decisions, nor is it optional for leaders who are for followers of Christ to refrain from making decisions."

**Dennis Bakke - Founder and former CEO of AES,**

**author of national bestseller Joy at Work.**

"When I went into business, I always wanted to incorporate giving into whatever I did... [TOMS Shoes has] allowed me to go into ministry without having to leave my passion for entrepreneurialism."

**Blake Mycoskie - Founder and Chief Shoe Giver of TOMS Shoes**

"When I go into a new venue, I try to be transparent about my faith and values in a non-offensive way. This sets the bar of expectations for how I will conduct myself. This then allows me to use others to hold myself accountable."

**Steve Lynn – Founder and CEO of Backyard Burgers**

"If I could give one piece of advice...it is to find a small group of confidants with whom you can share [genuine] relationship. It will be beneficial to you throughout your career and throughout your life."

**Edwin Meese III – 75th Attorney General of the United States of America**

"We are a faith-friendly organization that gives permission for all faiths...People ask how justify the cost of a workplace chaplaincy program...There's now enough measured evidence to demonstrate that plants are healthier because we have these ministers around to take on some tough issues."

**John Tyson – Chairman and former CEO of Tyson Foods**

EXPLORE AT WWW.RUSSELL-MEDIA.COM

find out more about Business As Mission (BAM), through . . .

**the MISSIONAL ENTREPRENEUR**
*Principles and Practices for Business as Mission*